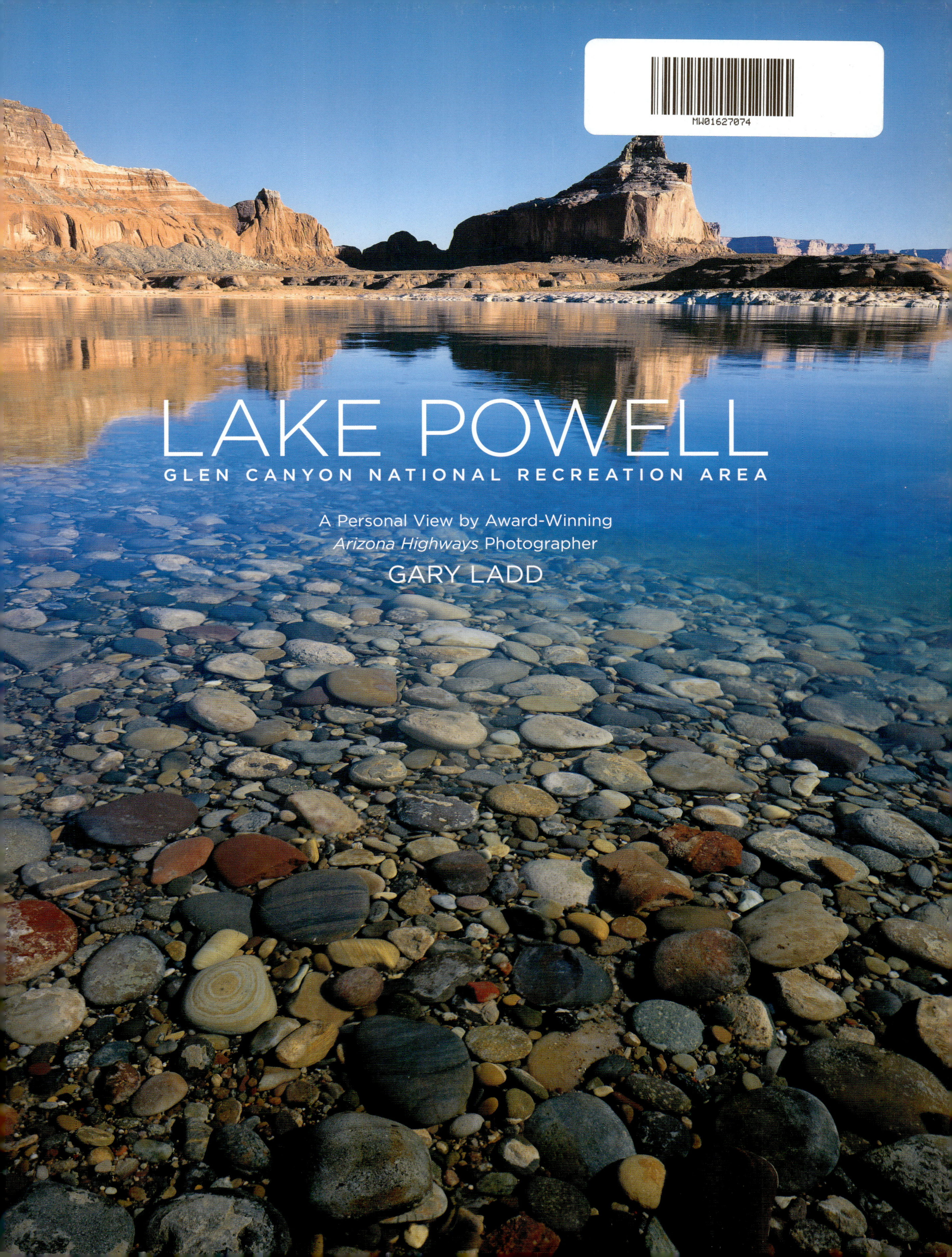
MW01627074
LAKE POWELL
GLEN CANYON NATIONAL RECREATION AREA
A Personal View by Award-Winning
*Arizona Highways* Photographer
GARY LADD

Book Designer: MARY WINKELMAN VELGOS
Book Editor: RANDY SUMMERLIN
Copy Editor: BETH DEVENY
Photography Editor: JEFF KIDA
Map: KEVIN KIBSEY
Creative Director: BARBARA GLYNN DENNEY

Text and photographs by Gary Ladd. Most of the photographs appearing in this book were made with a 4x5 field camera and film. Digital capture was not employed.

Preface: *A Passion for the Landscape* by Joe Alston

© 2010, Arizona Department of Transportation, State of Arizona

All rights reserved.

Except for quotations used in articles, reviews, and book listings, no part of this book may be reproduced in any form by any electronic or mechanicals means, including information storage and retrieval systems, without written permission from *Arizona Highways*.

Library of Congress Control Number: 2009938978
ISBN 978-0-9822788-3-3
First printing, 2010
Printed in China.

Published by the Book Division of *Arizona Highways* magazine, a monthly publication of the Arizona Department of Transportation, 2039 West Lewis Avenue, Phoenix, Arizona 85009.
Telephone: (602) 712-2200
Web site: www.arizonahighways.com

Publisher: WIN HOLDEN
Editor: ROBERT STIEVE
Senior Editor/Books: RANDY SUMMERLIN
Creative Director: BARBARA GLYNN DENNEY
Photography Editor: JEFF KIDA
Production Director: MICHAEL BIANCHI
Production Coordinator: ANNETTE PHARES

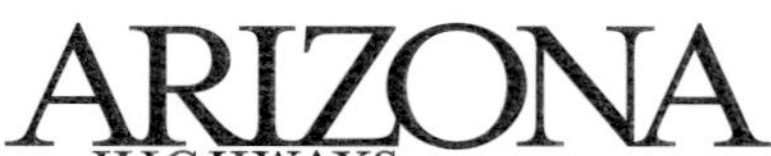


Title Page: **River cobbles armor the shoreline** of an ephemeral island near the south shore of Padre Bay. The cobbles were stranded on a gravel bar tens of thousands of years ago, left behind by the ancient Colorado River before it carved deep into the land to create modern Glen Canyon. Boundary Butte, at the Arizona-Utah border, lies on the horizon.

Contents Page: **Falling lake levels in early March** trapped a pool of lake water in a bedrock basin near Kane Wash. Lake Powell routinely loses elevation during late summer, fall, and winter. Snowmelt from the Rocky Mountains usually begins to bolster the lake's volume by mid-April.

# Contents

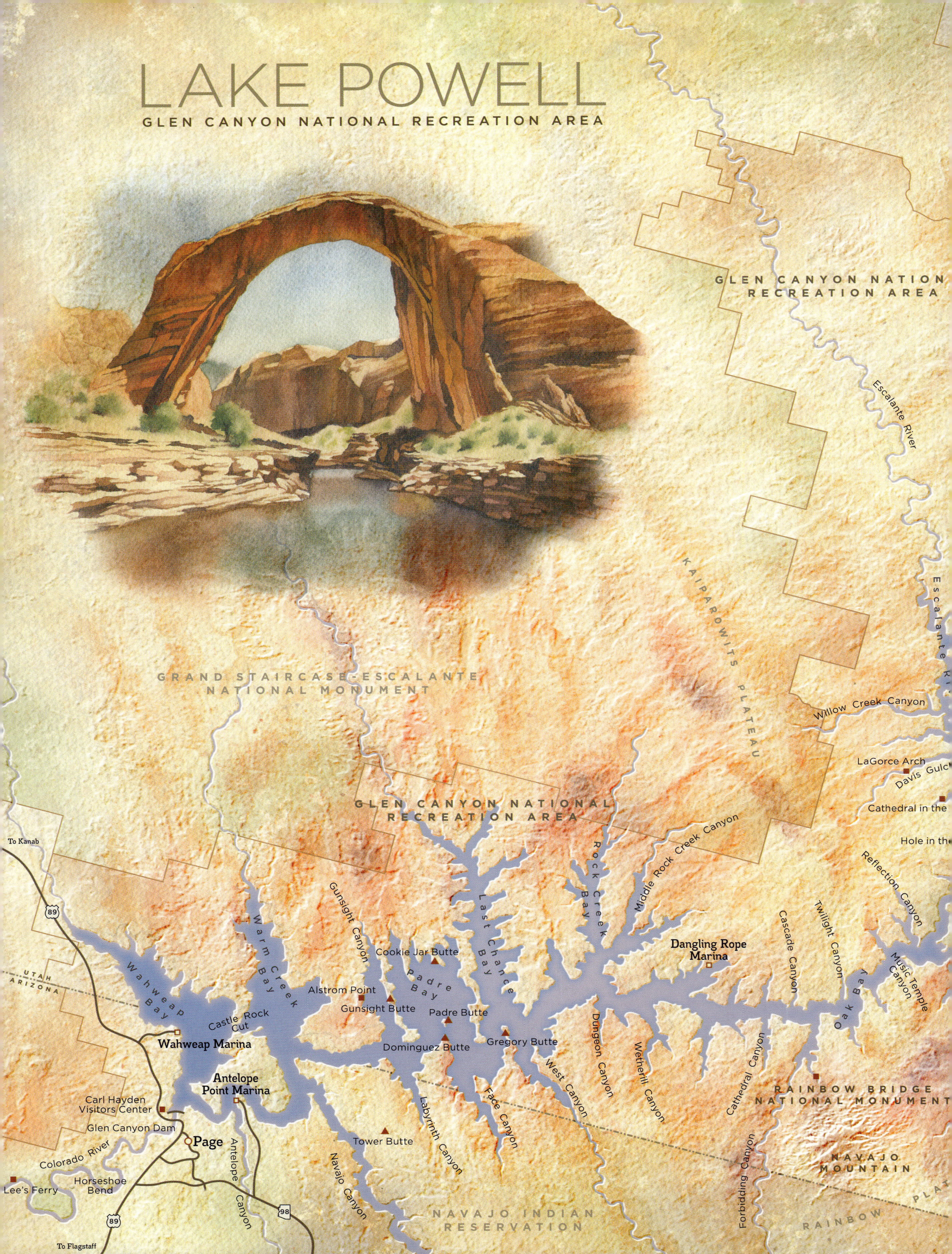
LAKE POWELL
GLEN CANYON NATIONAL RECREATION AREA
GLEN CANYON NATION
RECREATION AREA
Escalante River
KAIPAROWITS PLATEAU
Escalante Ri
GRAND STAIRCASE-ESCALANTE
NATIONAL MONUMENT
Willow Creek Canyon
LaGorce Arch
Davis Gulc
Cathedral in the
Hole in th
GLEN CANYON NATIONAL
RECREATION AREA
Middle Rock Creek Canyon
Rock Creek Bay
Reflection Canyon
To Kanab
89
Gunsight Canyon
Last Chance Bay
Cookie Jar Butte
Dangling Rope Marina
Cascade Canyon
Twilight Canyon
Music Temple Canyon
UTAH
ARIZONA
Wahweap Bay
Warm Creek Bay
Padre Bay
Alstrom Point
Gunsight Butte
Padre Butte
Castle Rock Cut
Oak Bay
Wahweap Marina
Dominguez Butte
Gregory Butte
Dungeon Canyon
Wetherill Canyon
Cathedral Canyon
Antelope Point Marina
West Canyon
RAINBOW BRIDGE
NATIONAL MONUMENT
Carl Hayden Visitors Center
Labyrinth Canyon
Face Canyon
Glen Canyon Dam
Colorado River
Page
Tower Butte
NAVAJO MOUNTAIN
Horseshoe Bend
Lee's Ferry
Antelope Canyon
Navajo Canyon
Forbidding Canyon
89
98
NAVAJO INDIAN
RESERVATION
RAINBOW
To Flagstaff

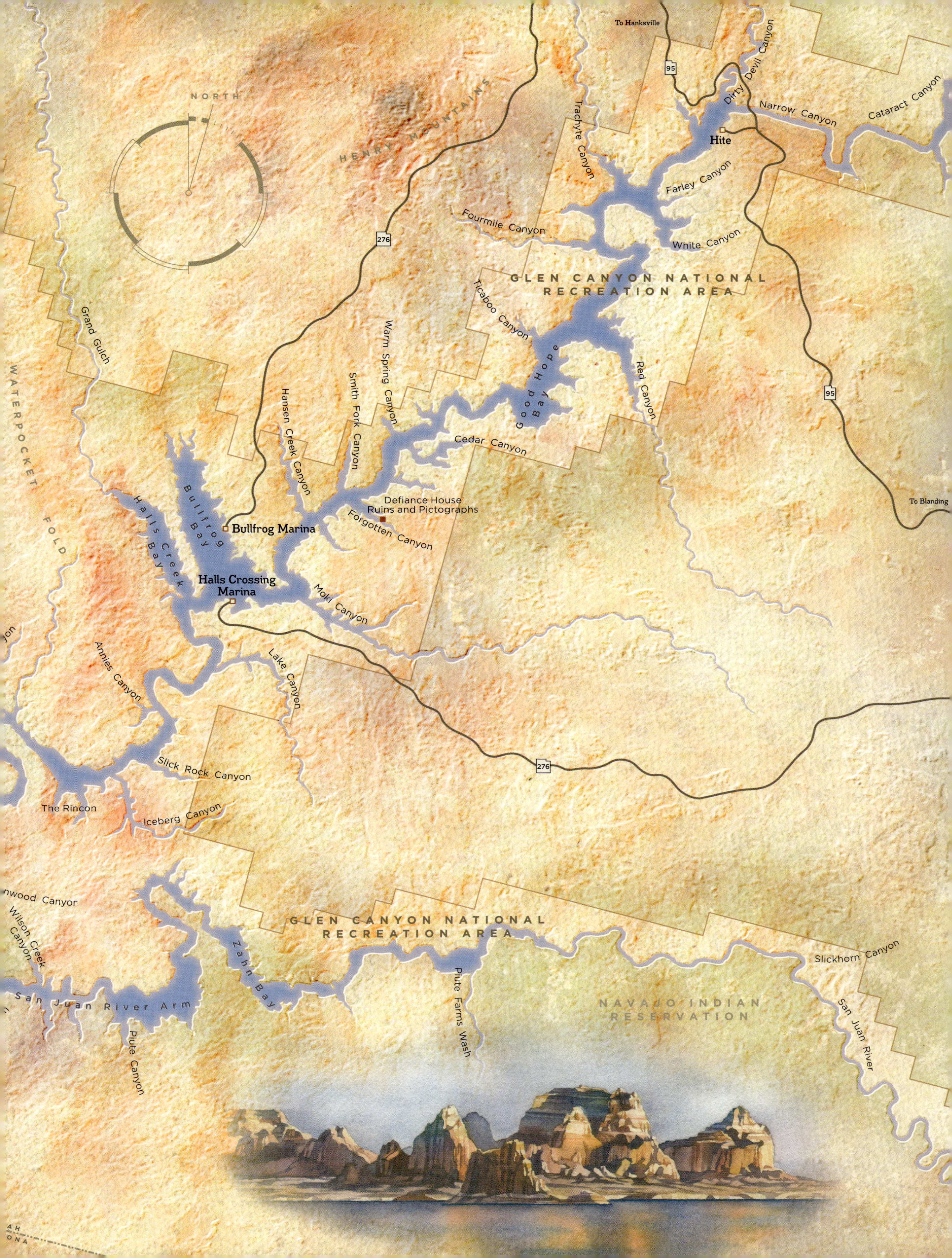

NORTH
HENRY MOUNTAINS
To Hanksville
95
Dirty Devil Canyon
Narrow Canyon
Cataract Canyon
Hite
Trachyte Canyon
Farley Canyon
Fourmile Canyon
White Canyon
276
GLEN CANYON NATIONAL
RECREATION AREA
Ticaboo Canyon
Good Hope Bay
Red Canyon
Grand Gulch
WATERPOCKET FOLD
Warm Spring Canyon
Smith Fork Canyon
Hansen Creek Canyon
Cedar Canyon
95
To Blanding
Bullfrog Bay
Halls Creek Bay
Defiance House
Ruins and Pictographs
Bullfrog Marina
Forgotten Canyon
Halls Crossing
Marina
Moki Canyon
Annies Canyon
Lake Canyon
276
Slick Rock Canyon
The Rincon
Iceberg Canyon
Wilson Creek
Canyon
GLEN CANYON NATIONAL
RECREATION AREA
Zahn Bay
San Juan River Arm
Piute Farms Wash
Slickhorn Canyon
NAVAJO INDIAN
RESERVATION
San Juan River
Piute Canyon

# A Passion for the Landscape

*by Joe Alston*

In 1994, while settling into my new office at the Glen Canyon National Recreation Area headquarters building in Page, Arizona, one of the first things I noticed was a large-format photograph on the wall. It was a winter scene of Gunsight Butte and Padre Bay on Lake Powell. A fresh layer of snow covered the imposing sandstone formations under the broken clouds of a passing storm and wisps of steam rose from the lake in the early morning cold. The image was an unexpected and striking contrast to the houseboats, jet skis, and marinas on Lake Powell featured in the marketing brochures that had been included in my "Welcome to Page" packet. This stunning photograph was my introduction to Gary Ladd.

As the months and years passed, Gary became a friend and hiking companion. Occasionally, I accompanied him as he scouted for new photography locations or filled in a few remaining gaps in his personal exploration of Glen Canyon, Marble Canyon, and the Navajo Nation. Gary's off-trail routes are not for the fainthearted, and as he was choosing that next step up or across, I sometimes had to remind him that his legs were at least two inches longer than mine.

We scrambled, leaped, climbed, and crawled in places where a misstep would lead to disaster, but we were always rewarded for our efforts. We encountered prayer rocks left by canyon inhabitants, petroglyphs and Moki steps, early explorers' inscriptions, relics left by Civilian Conservation Corps workers, old hogans, helicopter crash remnants, snakes, and, if luck was with us, a setting for another perfect Gary Ladd photograph. Often, our discoveries would inspire Gary to launch into an impromptu history or geology lesson.

While these trips were personally gratifying, they also helped me appreciate the effort that Gary puts into both scouting for his images and developing an understanding of his subjects. When I now view one of his photos, not only do I admire the artistry and technique involved, I also appreciate the many predawn and post-sunset hours of backpacking — with a 4x5 camera, tripod, and film boxes through rugged and unforgiving country — that were required to produce the image. Gary will tell you his photos capture what is "seen through the camera window." It is not luck that his camera window ends up in the right place at the right time.

For the past 25 years, Gary has photographed the landscapes of the Southwest, from the intimate to the grand. He has focused his work on Glen Canyon National Recreation Area, and many of his photos capture Lake Powell in fiery sunrises, torrential monsoons, and sunsets of remarkable proportions. Gary has found and photographed the forgotten Glen Canyon beyond the lake. He has photographed the redbuds and fern glens, arches and bridges, and the reflections in pools after the rain.

As a former National Park Service land manager, it is my firm belief that all of our public lands, including Glen Canyon and the public lands surrounding it, are preserved because of the support of ardent users and visitors. I hope that you, the reader of this book, will appreciate the passion and respect Gary Ladd and many others have for these remarkable landscapes. I hope you will be moved to experience the pleasure of exploring these areas on your own and find them worthy of your support.

*Now retired, Joe Alston has served as superintendent of Grand Canyon National Park, Glen Canyon National Recreation Area-Rainbow Bridge National Monument, and Curecanti National Recreation Area. He was deputy superintendent at Yellowstone National Park and has worked as a park wrangler, ranger, and firefighter.*

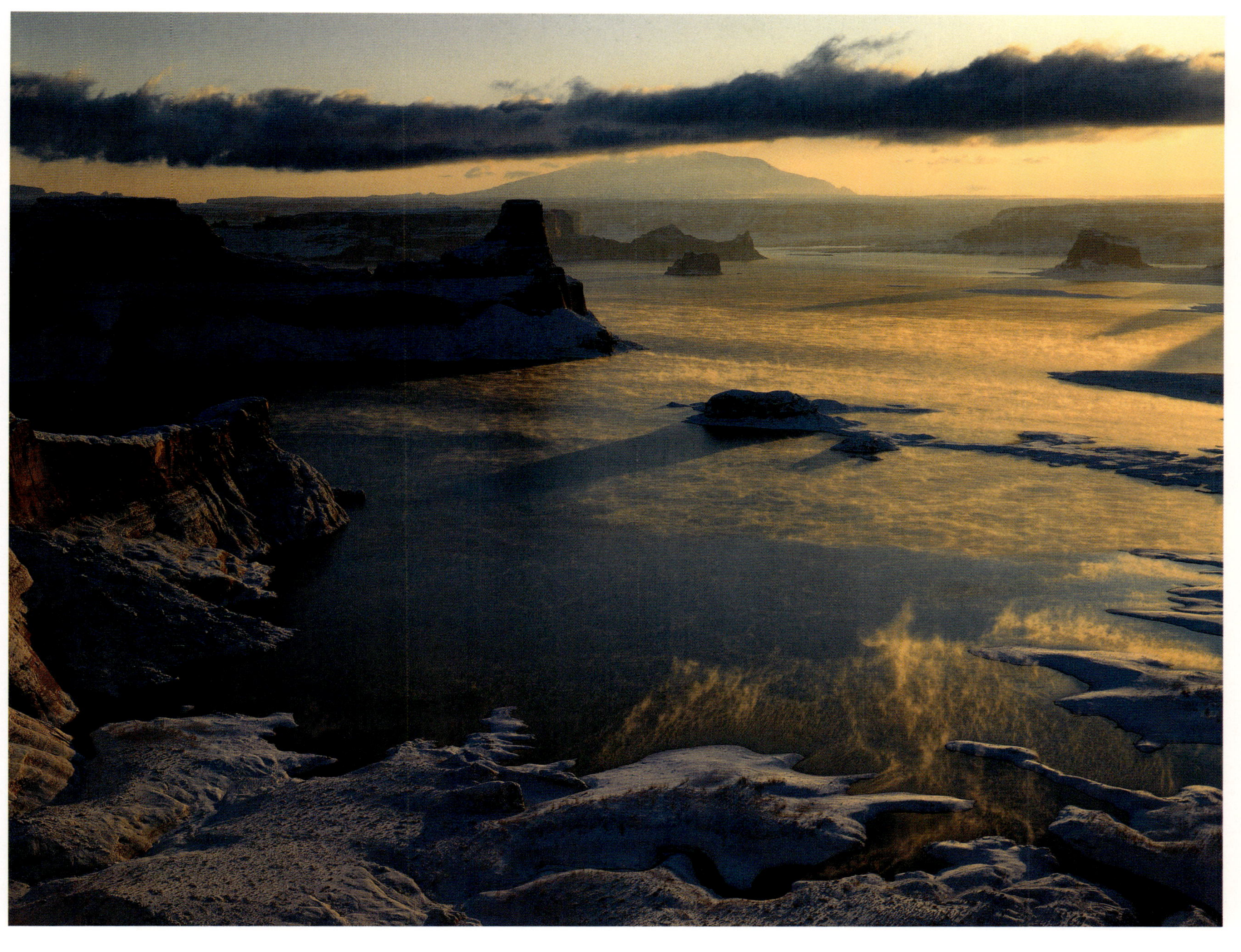

**A snowy Gunsight Butte** looms over Padre Bay on a cold sunrise in mid-January. Wisps of steam float across the water's surface while long shadows contract toward their originals. The view from Alstrom Point, a thousand feet above the lake, is accessible only by a long, often-rutted, partly sandy, unpredictable back-country road — and, in the case of this photograph, a chilly overnight campout.

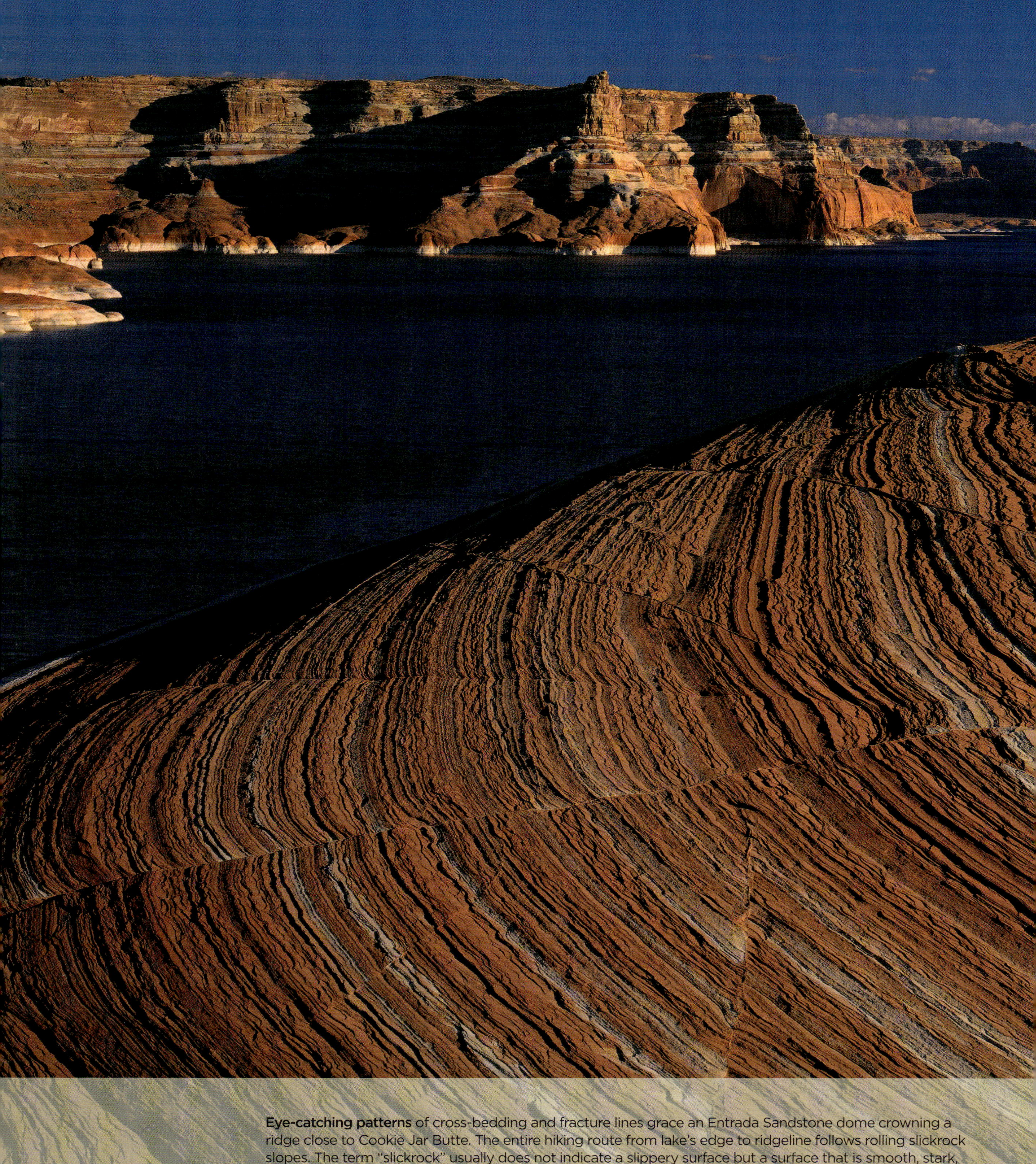

**Eye-catching patterns** of cross-bedding and fracture lines grace an Entrada Sandstone dome crowning a ridge close to Cookie Jar Butte. The entire hiking route from lake's edge to ridgeline follows rolling slickrock slopes. The term "slickrock" usually does not indicate a slippery surface but a surface that is smooth, stark, and undulating.

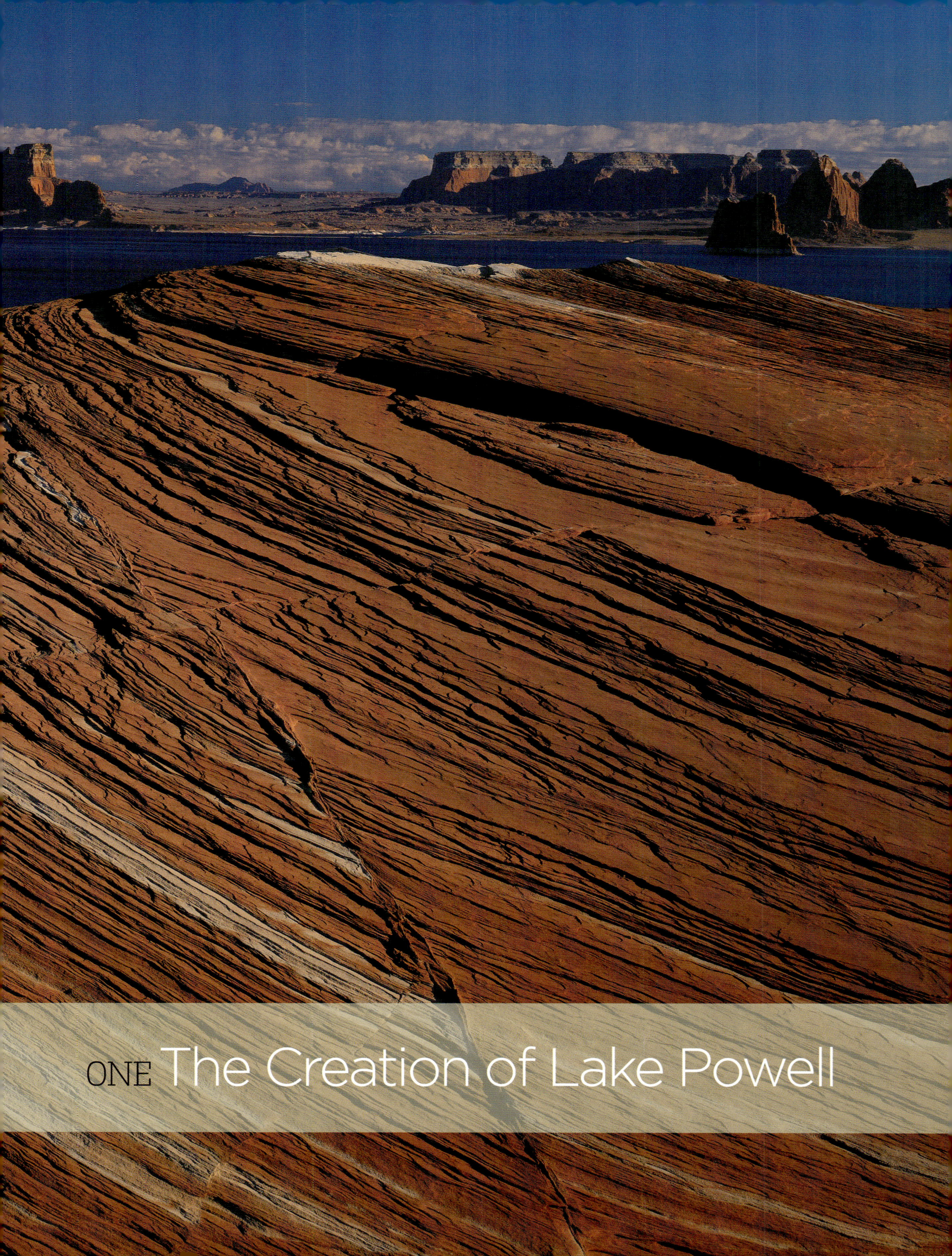

# ONE The Creation of Lake Powell

# ONE The Creation of Lake Powell

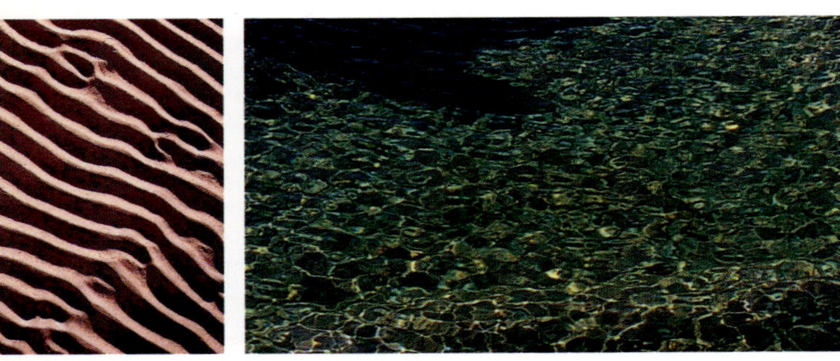
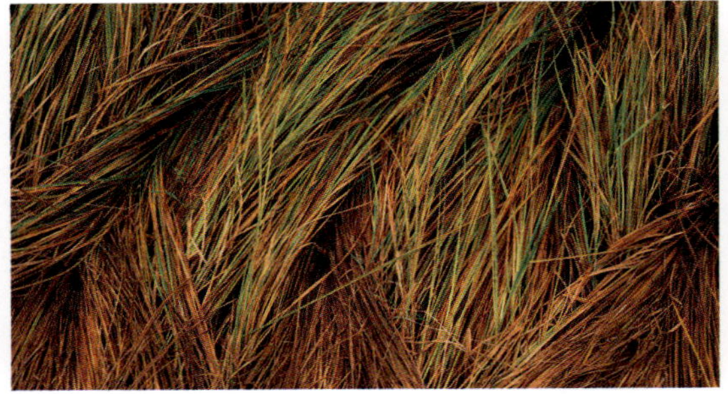
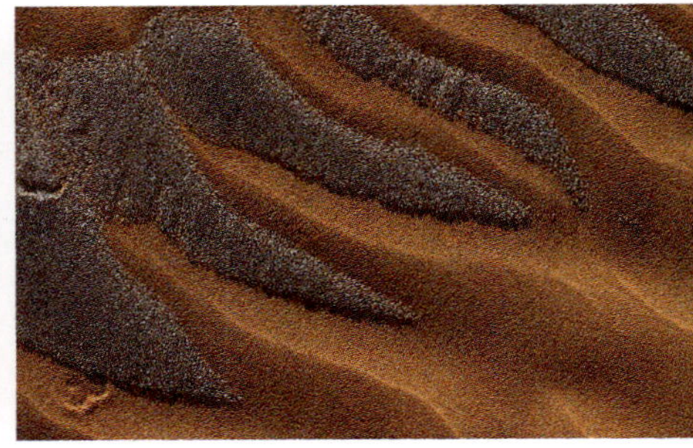

IN SEPTEMBER 1976, I launched my wooden dory, *Tatahotso*, at Hite Marina at the north end of Lake Powell. At the time, I had seen little of the lake and, after years of reading descriptions, wanted to look into Glen Canyon's mythic side canyons. I rowed the length of the lake alone, ducking into Forgotten Canyon, Davis Gulch, Hidden Passage, Music Temple Canyon, Forbidding Canyon, Rainbow Bridge Canyon, and many others.

By the time I tied up at the dock at Wahweap Marina, 150 miles and nineteen days later, I was hooked. The lake and the sandstone terrain's jaw-dropping physical beauty, the historical intricacies of unlikely human endeavors there, and the stately geology of Glen Canyon National Recreation Area were almost beyond belief. I'd be back. Thirty-five years later, after a couple hundred additional lake explorations, I'm still in awe.

Time broadens one's perspectives. Today, I'm both dazzled and disconcerted by Lake Powell. Like most other massive projects made possible by advances in technology and civilization's encroachment on the natural world, Lake Powell presents us with a double-edged sword. It offers both blessings and worrisome unintended consequences. Its unique mix of "good" and "bad" generates a curious magnetism all its own. Lake Powell's full ambience — its size, its gifts, its issues, its beauty, its complexity — is genuinely humbling. How did all this get started?

Left to right: **Fossilized ripples** mark a sandstone slab near the mouth of White Canyon.
**Patterns of sunlight** dance across the bottom of a shallow pool in Face Canyon.
**Aquatic sedge** gets braided by fluctuating flows of the Colorado River.
**January frost** rapidly evaporates on rippled sands near Hansen Creek.

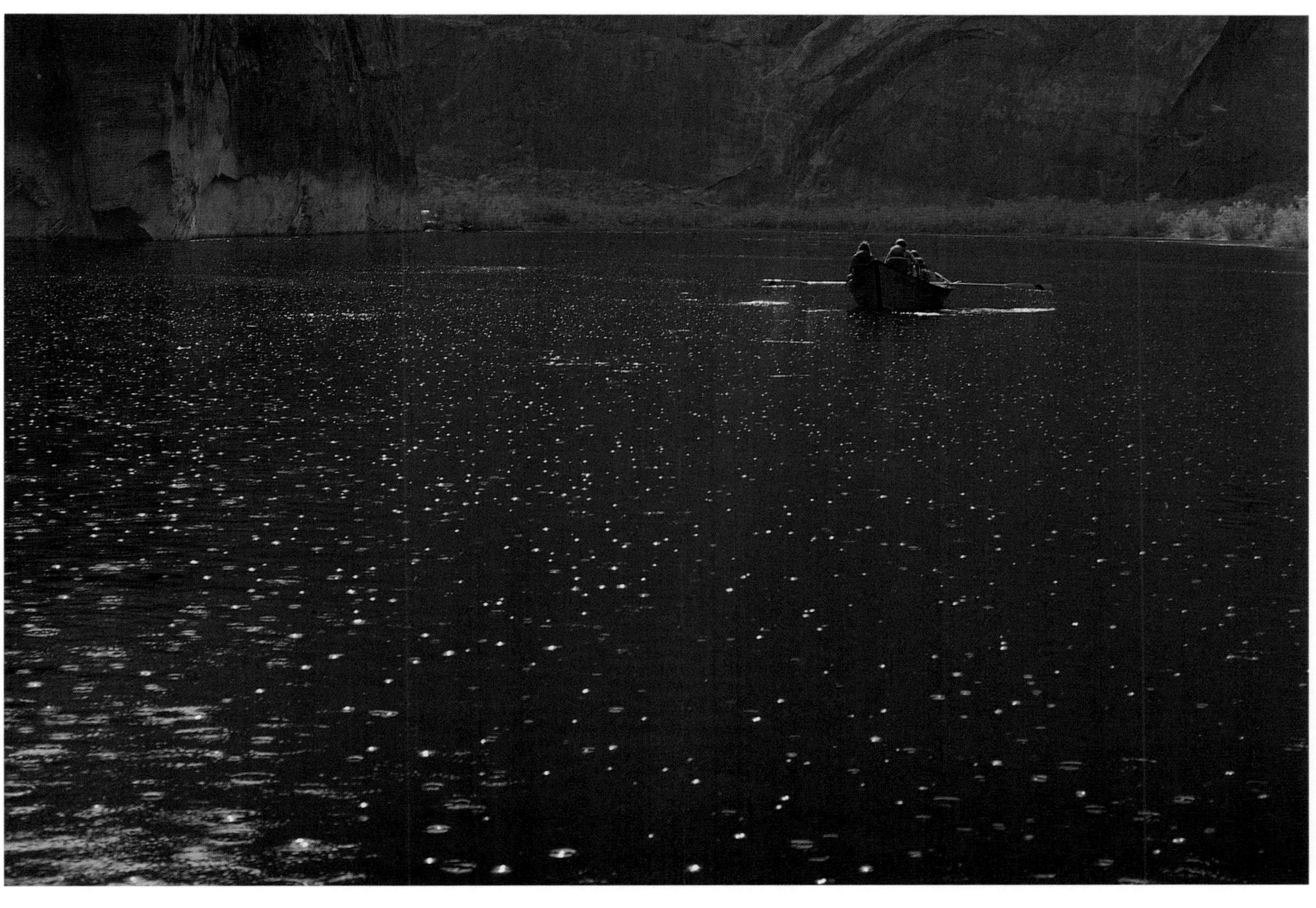

**A mid-July monsoon rain** speckles the Colorado River downstream from Glen Canyon Dam in the 15-mile surviving segment of "old" Glen Canyon. Since 1963, when the gates of the dam first closed, the Colorado River has routinely run clear and cold year-round and without its ancient annual rhythm of spring floods and summer lows. The dam-wrought changes have reshaped river corridor plant and animal populations.

## Intents and Purposes

In October 1956, President Dwight D. Eisenhower, seated in Washington, D.C., pushed a button setting off the first explosive blast at a dam site in Glen Canyon, Arizona, more than 2,000 miles away. Seven years of construction followed while Glen Canyon Dam, its power plant, transmission lines, a hundred miles of new highway, a soaring steel arch bridge across the Colorado River, and the town of Page were fashioned from the desert wilderness.

Glen Canyon Dam's primary purpose is to store Colorado River water. During periods of high flows, usually in the form of spring snowmelt runoff from the Rocky Mountains, the dam hoards excess water in its reservoir, Lake Powell. In dry months and years, the water is released to downstream users who might otherwise receive little. Control of the river allows the states bordering the upper Colorado River to withdraw large amounts of the river's flow for local purposes, while guaranteeing downstream water-users their share by setting free some of Lake Powell's storage.

As an added project benefit, Glen Canyon Dam's power plant generates electricity from the fall of water from the lake to the river. Power sales repay the federal government for the dam's construction and maintenance along with other Colorado River reclamation projects. And Lake Powell's recreational activities have stimulated economic activity along the Arizona-Utah border that had been idling for decades.

More than 5 million cubic yards of concrete were required to build the dam and power plant. From the summer of 1960 until September 1963, pouring continued at a furious pace until Lem Wylie, the head of construction at Glen Canyon, tossed his battered hat into a cage of rebar on the crest of the dam to see it disappear beneath the final bucket of concrete.

The dam rises 710 feet from bedrock, just 16 feet shy of the height of Hoover Dam located downstream. Lake Powell, like Lake Mead behind Hoover Dam, has a maximum capacity of about two full years' flow of the Colorado River.

Today, an array of sensors monitors the dam to assure its continued safety. The Bureau of Reclamation keeps an eye on the dam using everything from a seismograph, strain gauges, piezometers, and lasers to five reassuringly simple 637-foot plumb lines.

## Costs and Benefits

Despite all that it delivers, Glen Canyon Dam also comes with baggage. Upstream from the dam, Lake Powell drowned an exquisite canyon. Downstream in Grand Canyon, the dam has completely reconstituted the river's character — its water temperature, sediment load, yearly flow regimen, riverside vegetation, and animals along the river corridor. For 440 miles, from the lake's upper reaches to the head of Lake Mead, the Colorado's natural riparian ecosystem has been thrown for a loop. Scientists continue to study the many effects of the dam and look for ways to mitigate those that are undesirable.

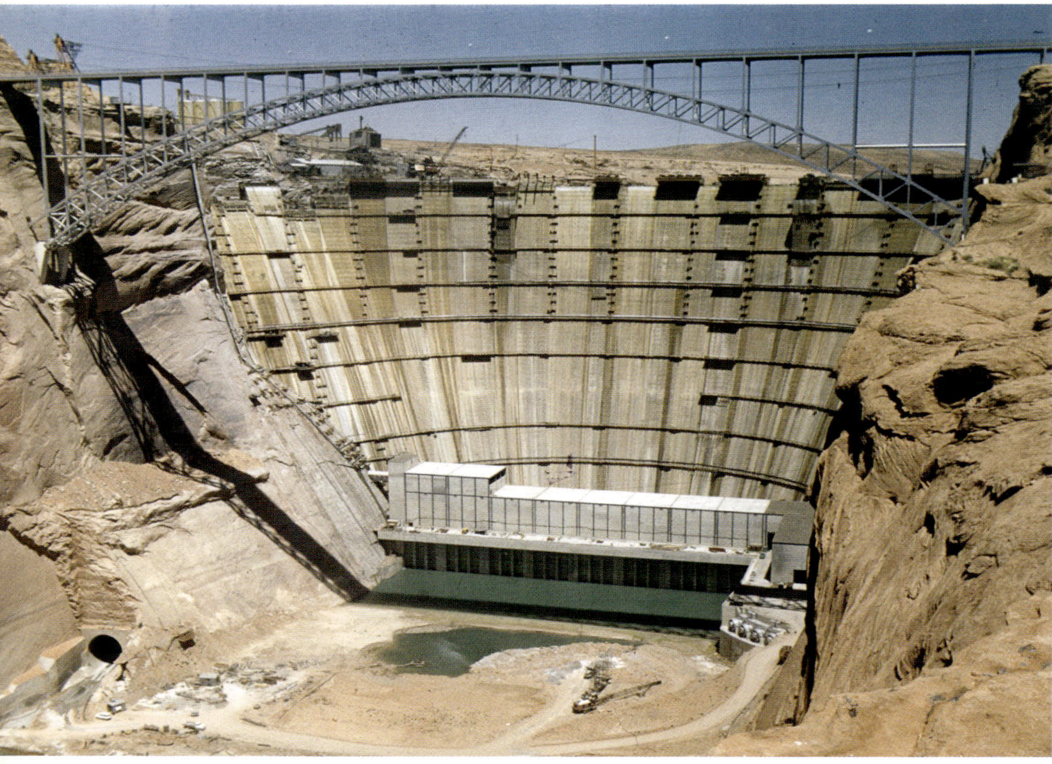

**In 1963,** the dam is nearing a "topping out." The west river diversion tunnel (at the lower left) has been closed, but the east tunnel (at the lower right but not visible) continues to reroute the Colorado around the damsite.

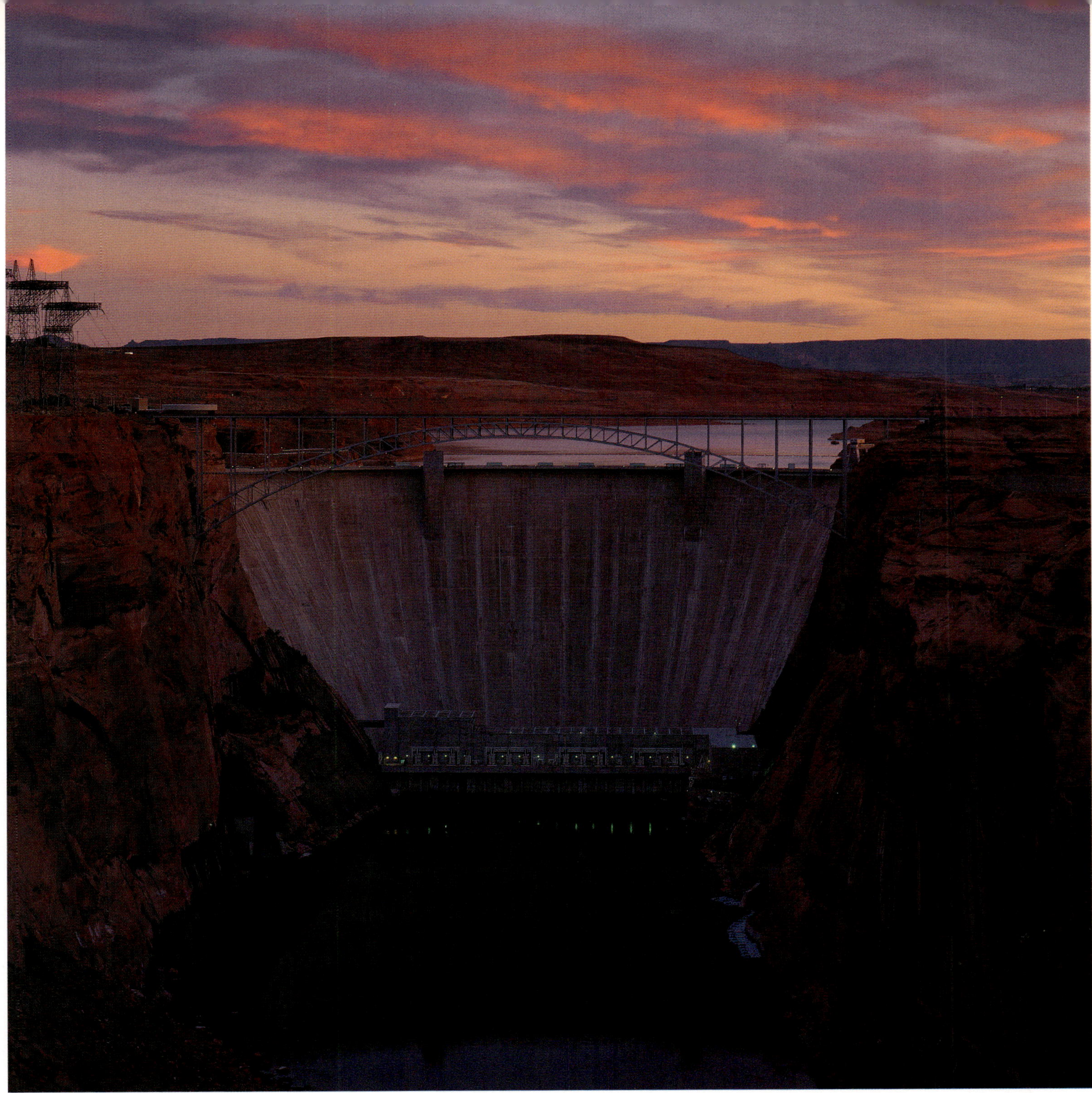

Most obvious of the dam's benefits are Lake Powell's incredible recreational opportunities: boating on a lake surrounded by magnificent vistas and authentic wilderness untouched by roads and habitation, back-packing in lonely side canyons, and the possibility of an escape from the crush of civilization.

Lake Powell is wonderful and dreadful, beautiful and horrifying, worthless and priceless, all depending upon which yardstick is used. To me, a frequent visitor, the place is just plain amazing and enchanting, a lake of paradoxes cradled in a slickrock wonderland.

**Glen Canyon Dam** is located in Arizona near the Utah border. It rises 710 feet from bedrock with a maximum thickness of 350 feet and contains almost 5 million cubic yards of concrete. The dam's mass of 10 million tons, along with its arch-shaped footprint locked into the canyon walls, assures that even the highest Lake Powell levels cannot budge it. The hydroelectric plant at its base can generate up to 1,320 megawatts of electricity.

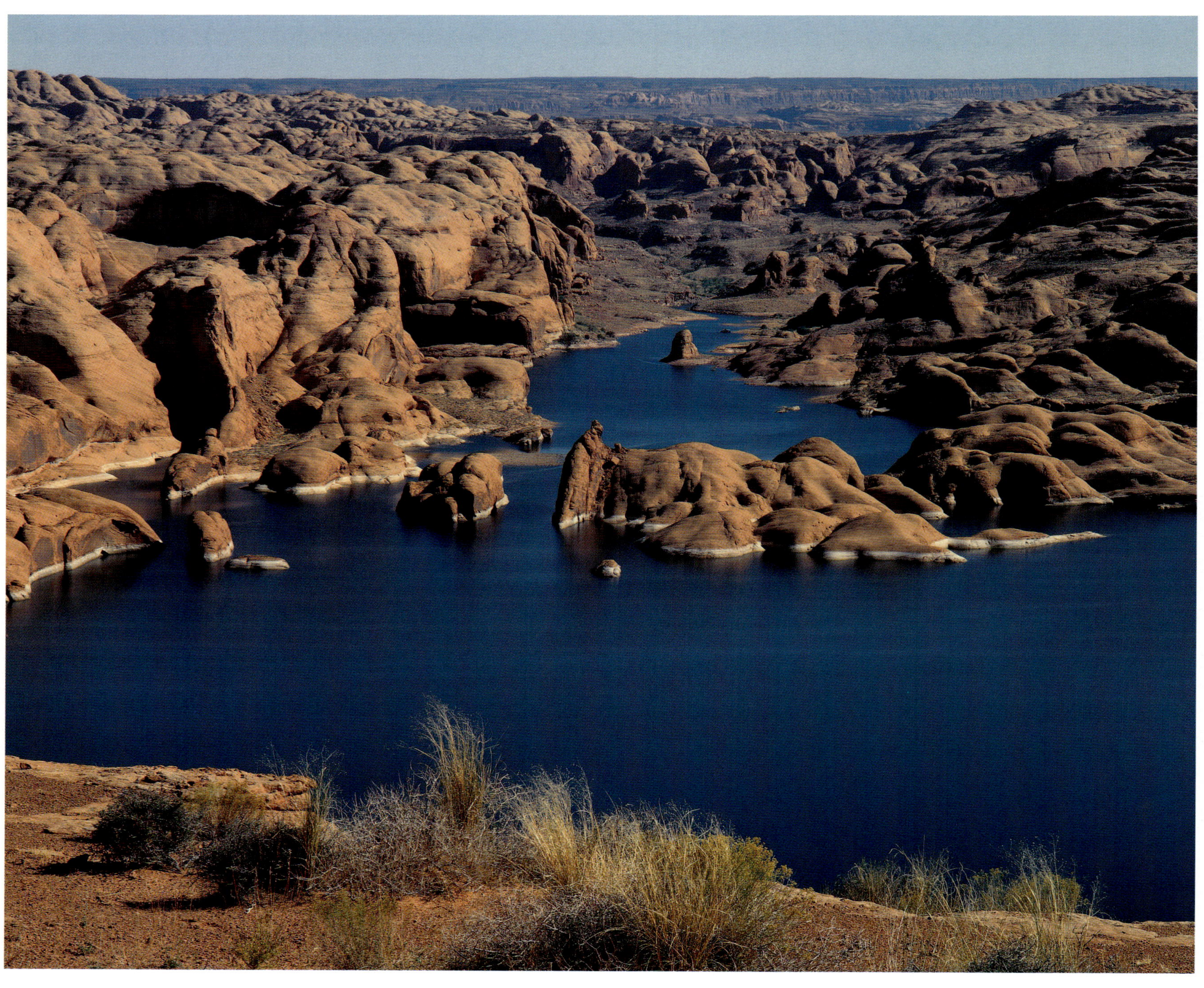

Above: **From the rim of Glen Canyon** near the top of Hole-in-the-Rock, the view to the east includes the Cottonwood Canyon arm of Lake Powell. In January 1880, after six weeks of digging and blasting, 250 Mormon pioneers skidded and drove 80 wagons down a 1,000-foot-deep cleft in the east wall of Glen Canyon — the "hole in the rock" — to the Colorado River. After ferrying across the river and three more months of back-breaking labor, the expedition founded the new town of Bluff City, now Bluff, Utah, on the San Juan River. The Hole-in-the-Rock expedition is among those celebrated in Western history.

Right: **The rooms and walls of Three Roof Ruin** were built and occupied by the Ancestral Puebloans about 800 years ago. Today it overlooks the Escalante Arm of Lake Powell. Boaters willing to climb the toehold trail are welcome to visit the restored and stabilized ruins where National Park Service exhibits explain what archaeologists have discovered about these vanished people.

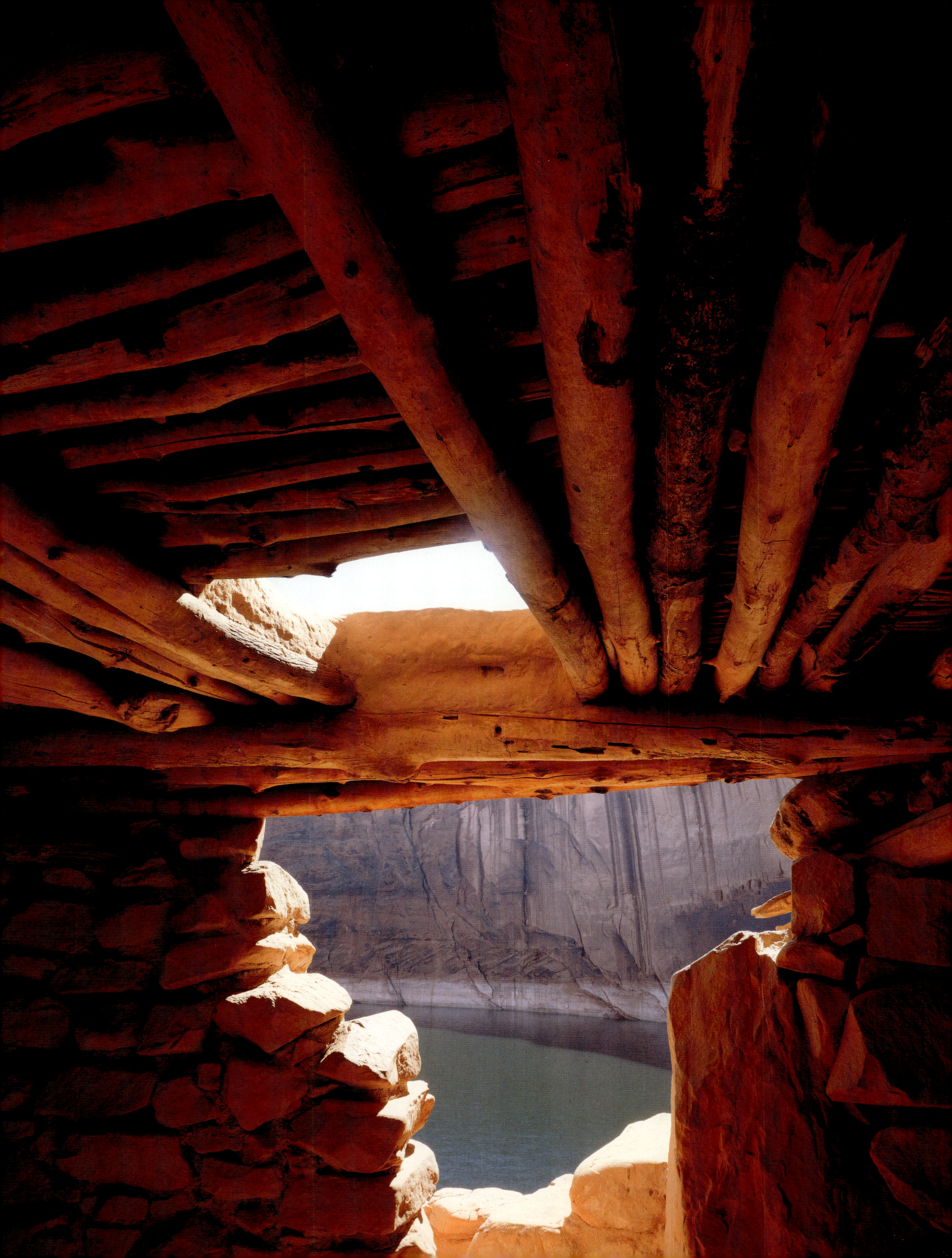

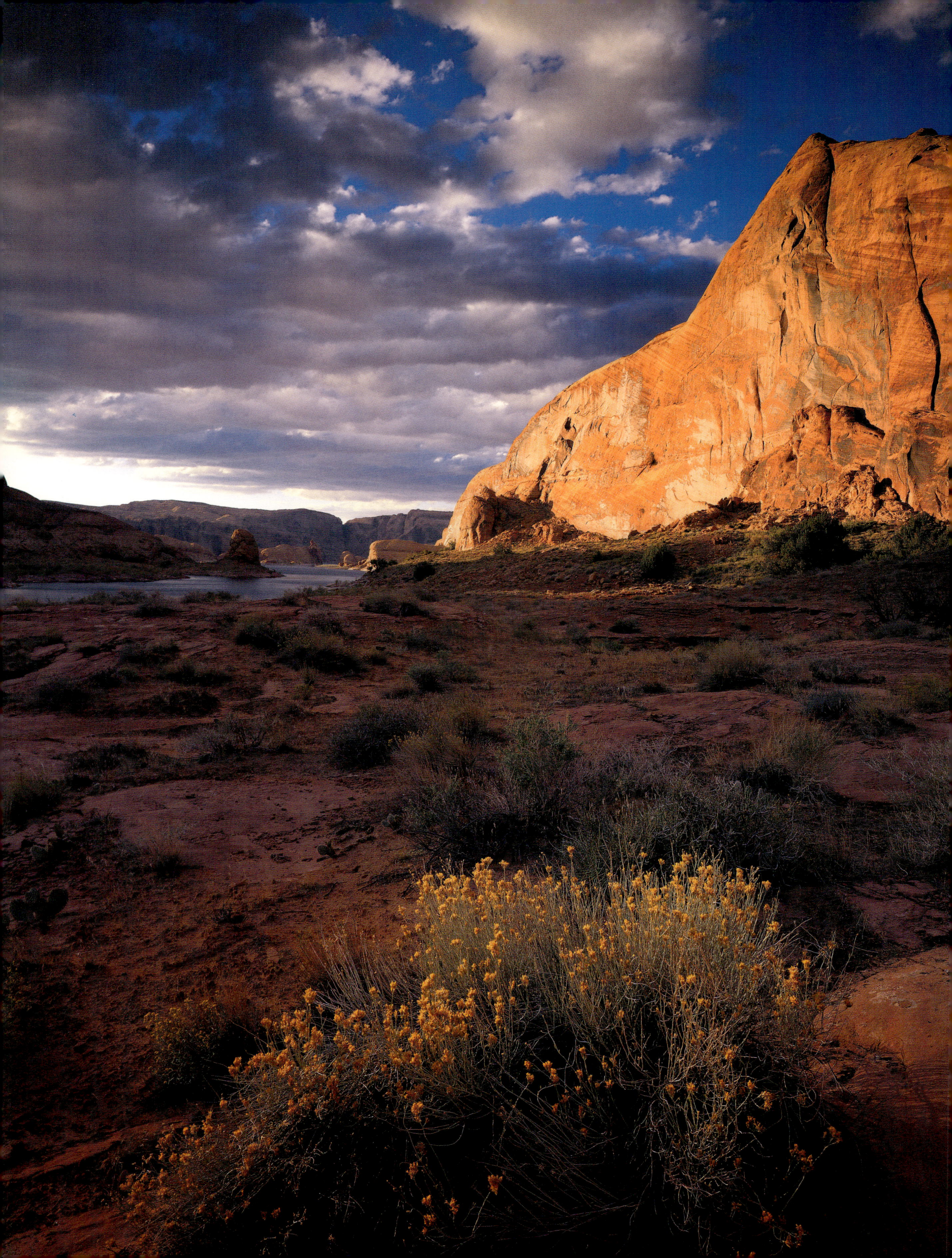

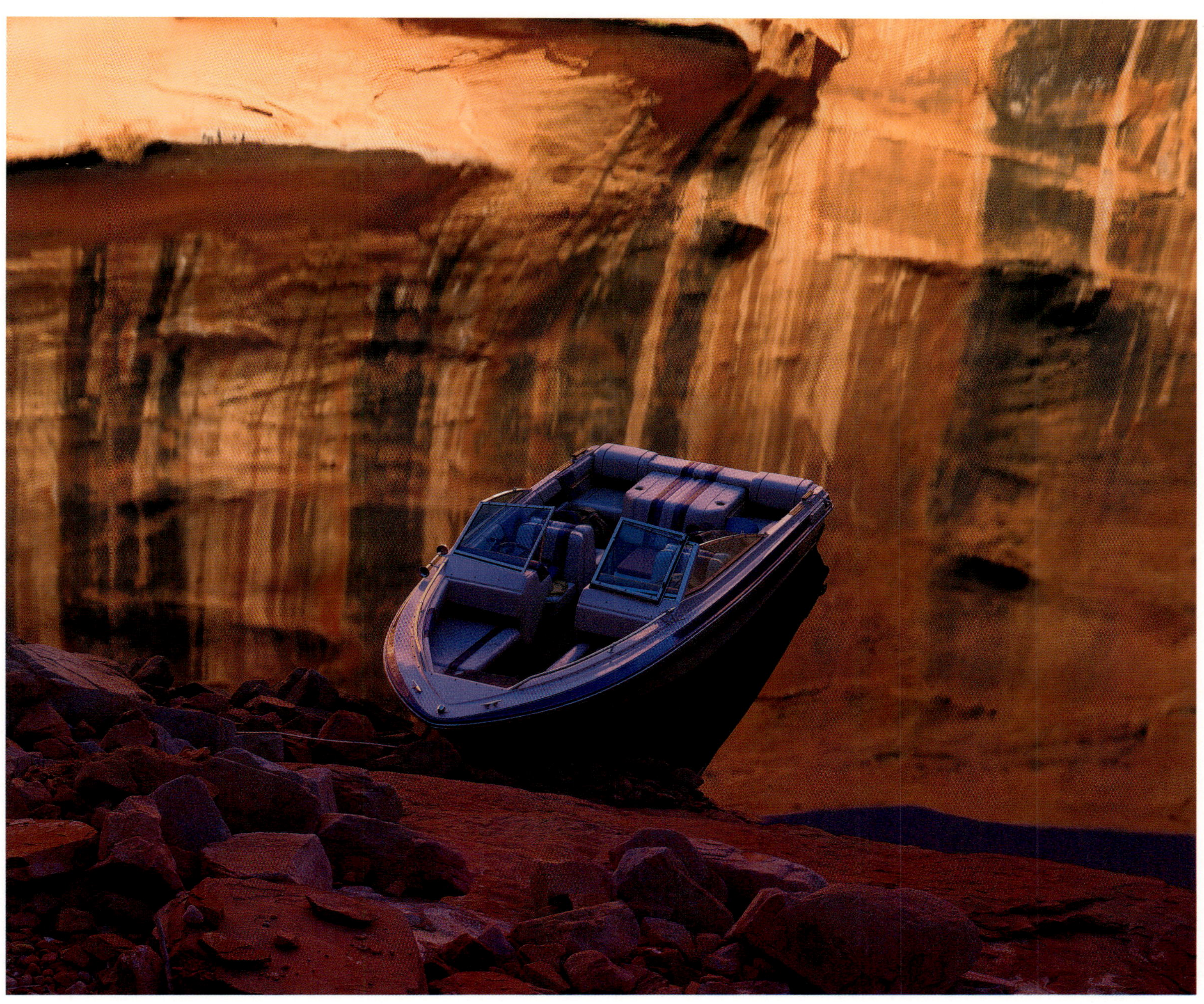

Left: **At most lake levels, Cottonwood Canyon** offers boaters both sandy beaches and miles of interesting hikes. On my first visit to the canyon, I hiked up to a divide that was labeled on my map as Aladdin's Lamp Pass. The name seemed peculiar until I arrived at the summit where a large rock formation looked exactly like an ancient oil lamp.

Above: **Reflections of desert varnish patterns** in Willow Canyon are so perfect that they appear to be solid rock supporting a boat. I made this photograph in December when few boaters disturb the surface of the lake and the silence of the surrounding canyons. The lake is nearly deserted in December, January, and February.

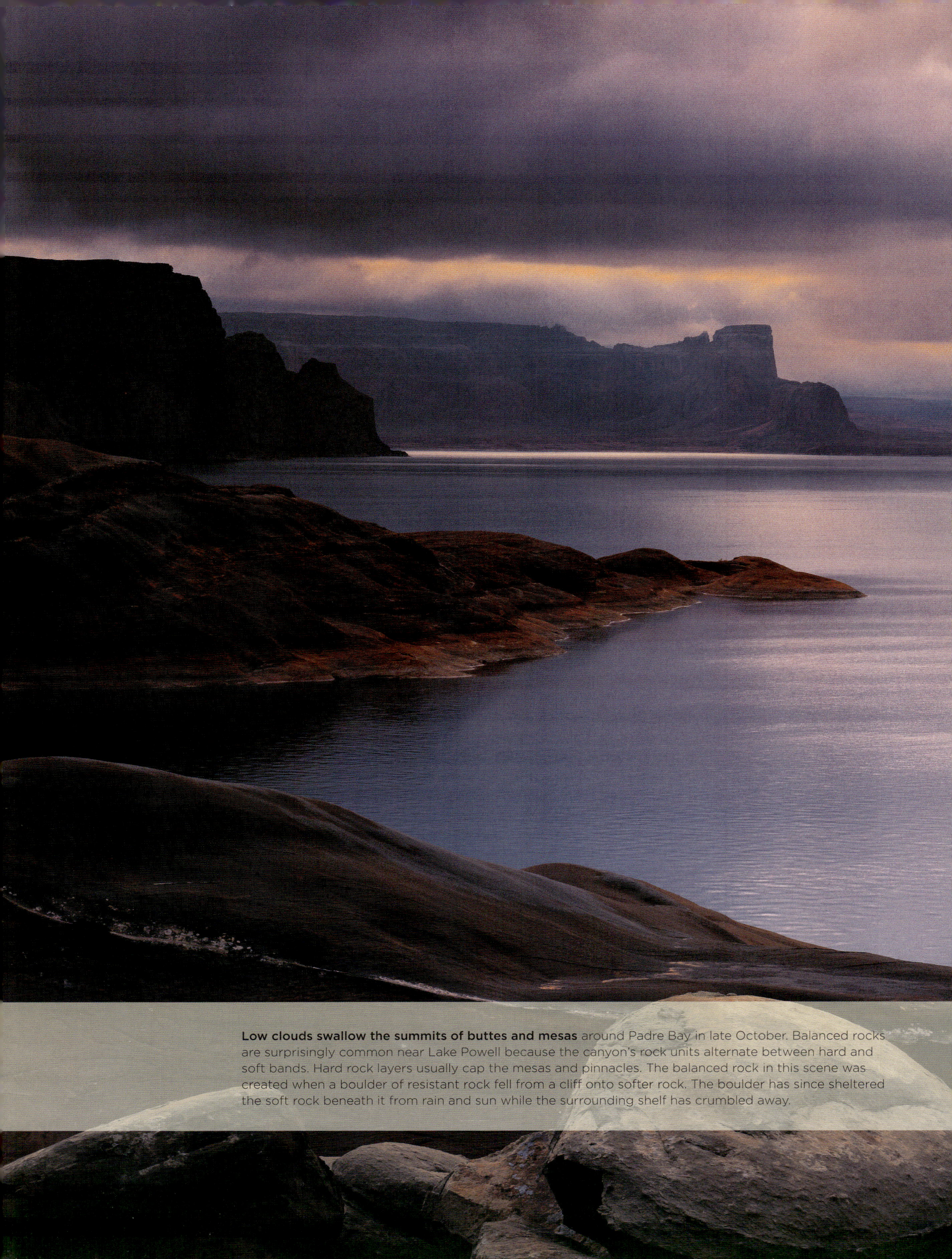

**Low clouds swallow the summits of buttes and mesas** around Padre Bay in late October. Balanced rocks are surprisingly common near Lake Powell because the canyon's rock units alternate between hard and soft bands. Hard rock layers usually cap the mesas and pinnacles. The balanced rock in this scene was created when a boulder of resistant rock fell from a cliff onto softer rock. The boulder has since sheltered the soft rock beneath it from rain and sun while the surrounding shelf has crumbled away.

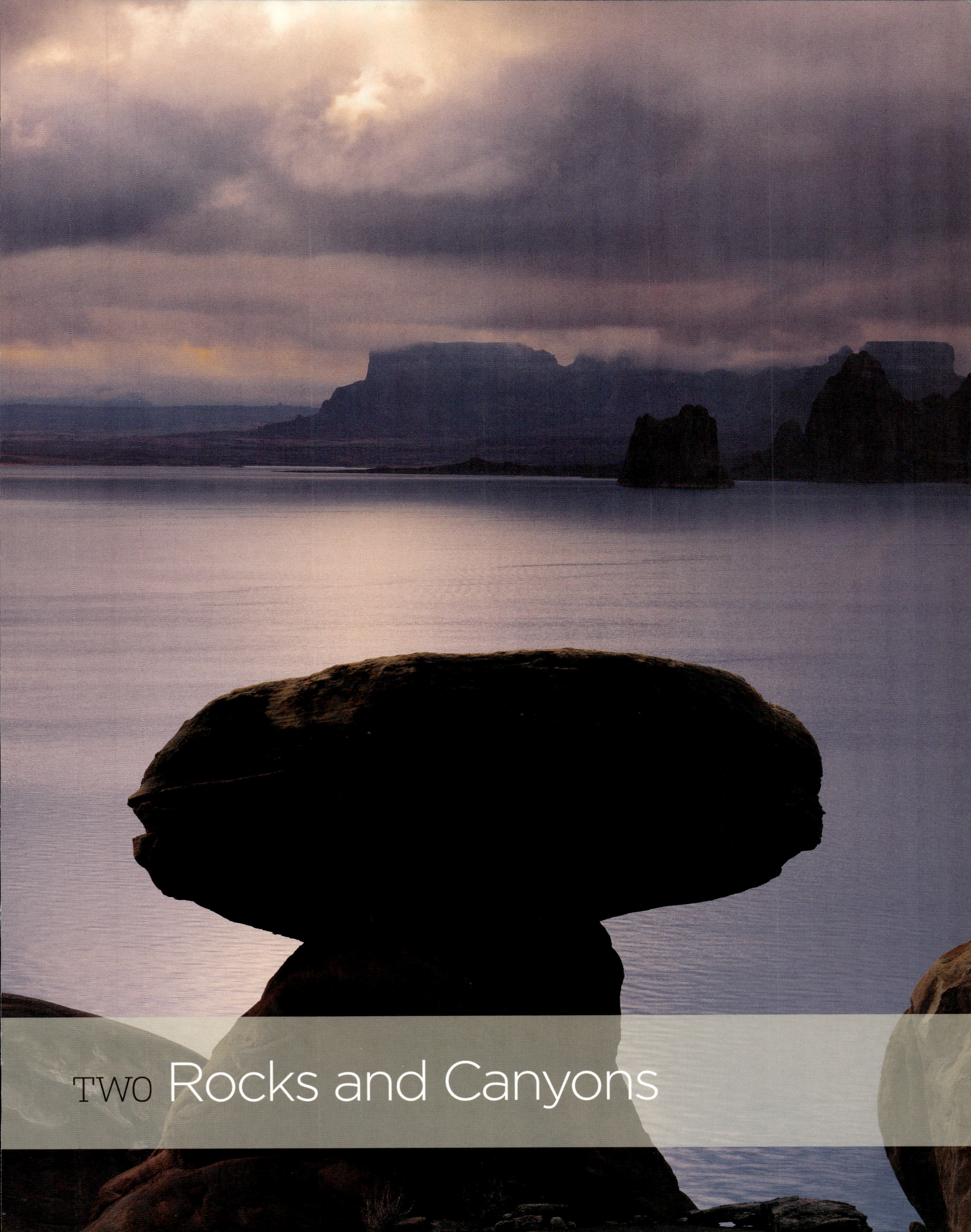

# TWO Rocks and Canyons

# TWO Rocks and Canyons

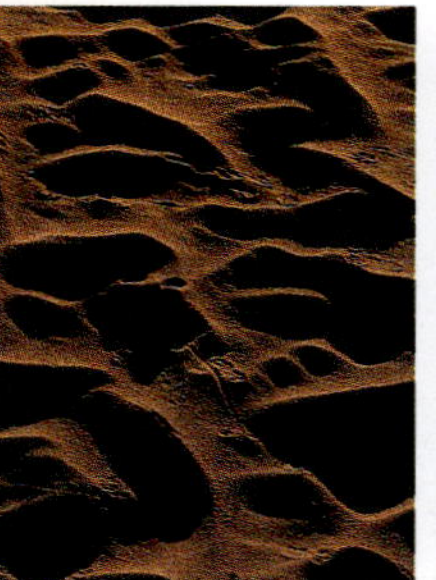
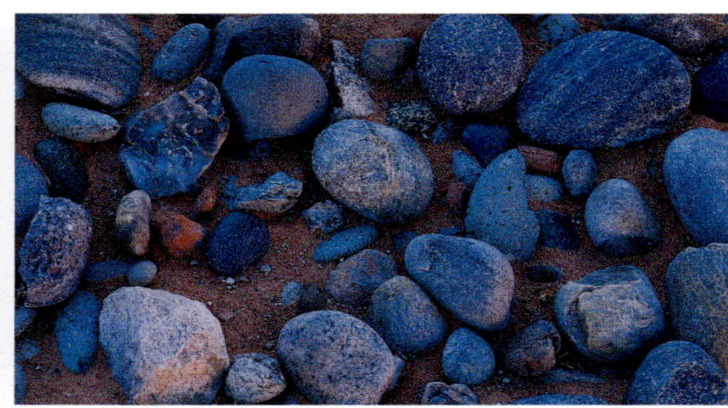
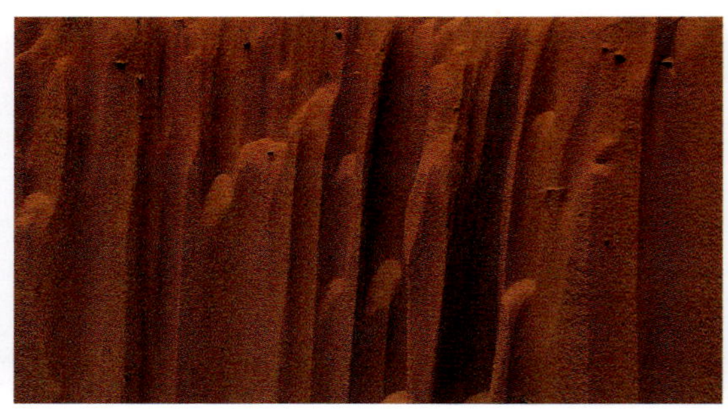
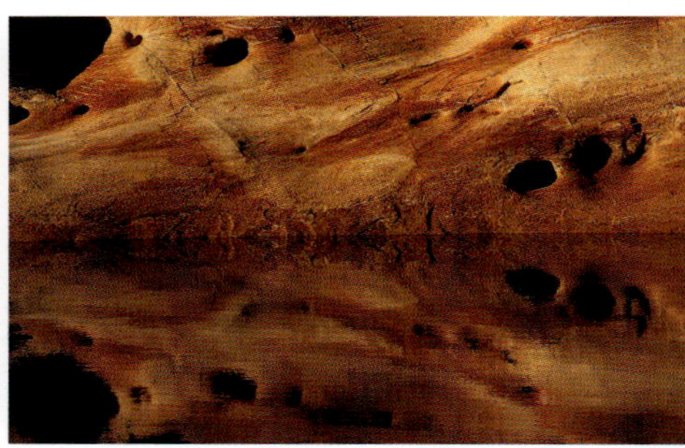

BEFORE ANTELOPE CANYON was designated a Navajo Tribal Park, before steel stairways were bolted to its walls, and before swarms of tourists arrived to stand awestruck in the magnificent slot canyon that is located just east of Page, Arizona, I often explored and photographed the canyon alone. On a summer day long ago, when no one was around, I reconnoitered along the canyon's east rim looking for a new point of entry. I found a notch where I could drop down onto a ledge that, surprisingly, led up-canyon into the dim interior. I wanted a fresh view of Antelope Canyon, and this might have been just the ticket.

My ledge soon dwindled to a sloping, narrow, low-ceilinged shelf requiring me to lie on my side and wiggle along. The wiggling was awkward but brief. The ledge flared out to a platform where I could stand and perhaps capture that new angle.

After a few minutes, however, I realized that this site was mediocre and not worth further trials. I packed up my gear, lay down at the ledge's gateway, and found that I could not execute a return trip on the sloping shelf. For reasons unclear, a right-side wiggle was way scarier than a left-side wiggle. I retreated to the platform, recomposed myself and tried again. Even worse.

From the platform I looked for another exit. I jumped the slot to a ledge on the west side. This new ledge led nowhere, neither up- nor down-canyon. Then, tension rising by the second, I stood on a knob and felt around on a ledge above me hoping to find a remedy, and not a rattlesnake. There was a crack, so I jammed my fingers into it and heaved myself up and was soon out on the rim.

No one knew of my whereabouts. No driver on State Route 98 could possibly hear my hollering. No one was likely to enter the canyon anytime soon. I was lucky to have escaped Glen Canyon's geology. Fortunately, time has given me ways to make sure this won't happen again — now that I'm older and *wider.*

Left to right: **Sand dune ripples** decorate Face Canyon.
**River cobbles are illuminated** by a clear blue winter sky.
**A sculptured sandbank** in Clear Creek Canyon appears hand-carved.
**The slickrock shoreline** of Last Chance Canyon is reflected in calm water.

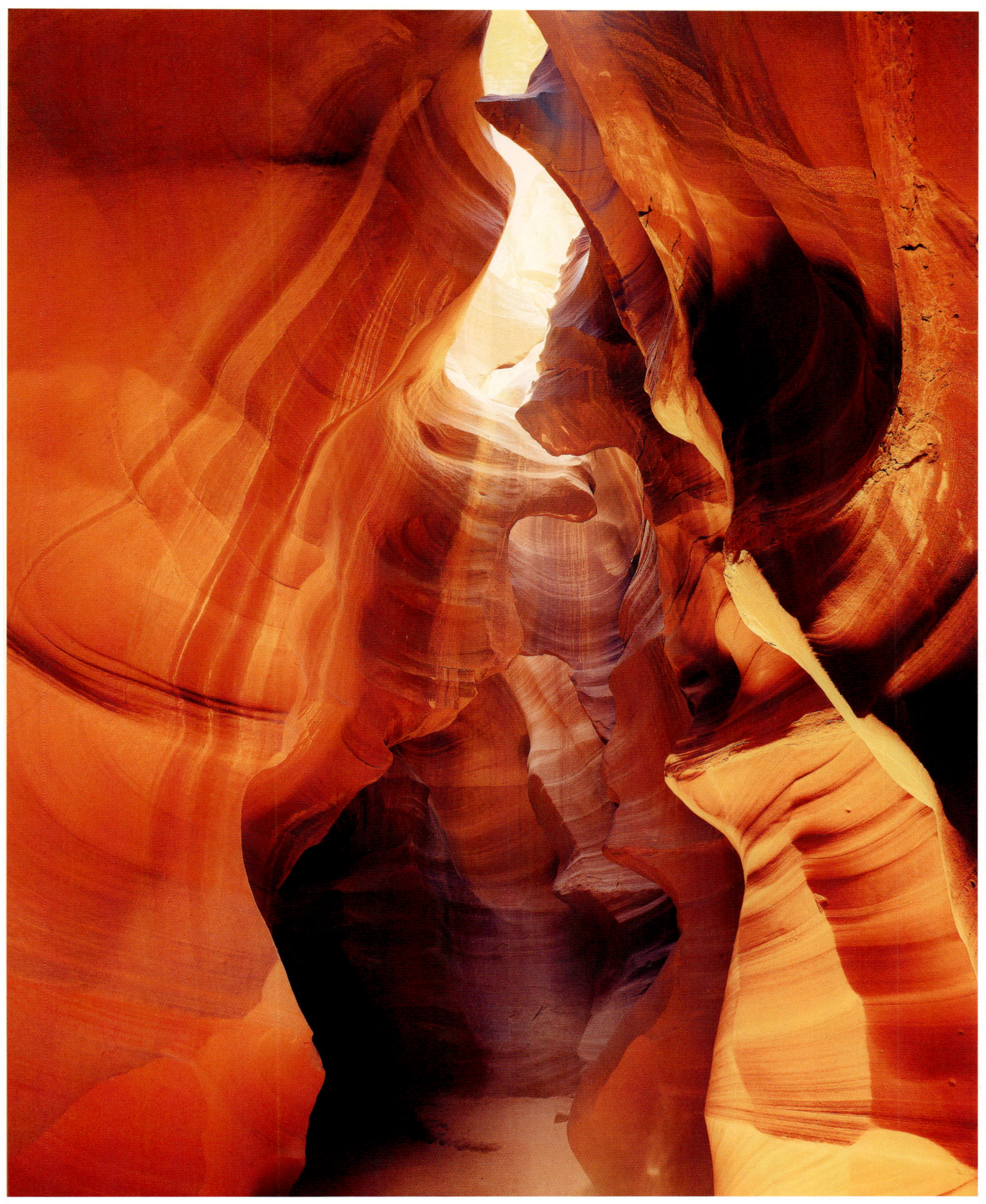

**The interlocking and overhanging walls** of Upper Antelope Canyon seemingly glow from within as sunlight is reflected upward from its sunlit floor. Slot canyons are carved fast and furiously when landslides, traveling sand dunes, rockfalls, and other geologic events force a drainage out of its bed to carve a new canyon. In the Glen Canyon area, awesome slot canyons are plentiful. But Upper Antelope Canyon possesses several photographer-friendly attributes: It's easy to walk through; it's not so deep that it's impossibly dark; it is highly sculptured; and its most photogenic section is comparatively long.

## Deposition, Then Canyon-Cutting

Like Grand Canyon, Glen Canyon possesses its own great stack of rocks. Glen Canyon's are younger. (That is, in most areas, Grand Canyon rock units are buried far beneath those of Glen Canyon's topography.) Most of the rock units in Grand Canyon and Glen Canyon were laid down during a half-billion-year period when this region was at low elevation — near, at, or just below sea level. During that time, the area slowly subsided while thousands of feet of silt, sand, and lime accumulated in the basin.

Beginning about 70 million years ago, the region's fortunes reversed — the thick sequence of rocks that had solidified in the basin began to rise, slowly at first, and faster more recently. Because of the uplift, the deposition of sediments halted and erosion assumed command. In the past few million years, erosion has gone wild; many hundreds of feet of rock have been scoured away by rain, freezing temperatures, the tug of gravity, and other processes as the land elevated.

The youngest and highest rock layers disappeared first. Thousands of feet of rock remain but even these have been deeply engraved by weathering and erosion.

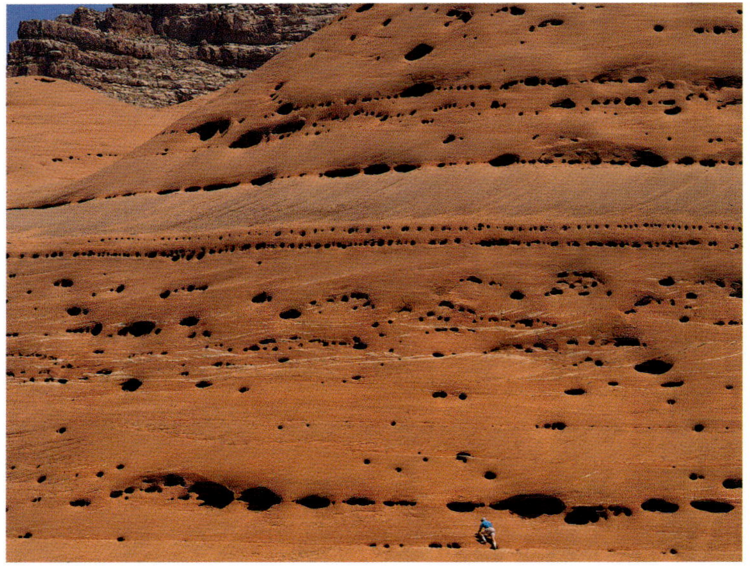

The Colorado River and its tributaries (along with earlier rivers that flowed here before the Colorado) did the carving and carting away. They sculpted and fashioned the landscape we see today — a canyon surrounded by buttes, mesas, and plateaus that are the remnants of the once-continuous rock layers that have been partially dismantled.

The unusual factor in this otherwise common geologic story is that during the uplift the horizontal posture of the sedimentary rock units was left intact. Typically, uplift brings with it faulting, tilting, and twisting. But not here. These rock units remain neat and tidy, creating today's coherent and aesthetically pleasing landscape.

## Glen Canyon Rock Units

Today, Navajo Sandstone dominates much of Lake Powell. Navajo Sandstone is often expressed in the form of high cliffs. It welcomes the formation of arches and bridges. And when it is exposed to vigorous flash floods, Navajo Sandstone erodes quickly to host sheer-walled slot canyons. In the Lake Powell region, the Navajo Sandstone measures about 1,100 to 1,200 feet thick.

Here and there around the lake, other rock units sometimes step into the limelight. Much of the Chinle Formation, for instance, is crumbly shale and wonderfully colorful. Both the Entrada Sandstone and Wingate Sandstone are often mistaken for Navajo Sandstone. All three are wind-deposited and warm in color, but the Entrada is younger and thinner, while the Wingate is older and far thinner.

The Glen Canyon area is an erosional wonderland. Much of what we see today has been carved and shaped in just the last 500,000 years. At this moment in geologic time, the Navajo Sandstone and its fellows lie near river level and lake level. In a few million years, if current regional uplift and erosion rates continue, Glen Canyon will be transformed, looking perhaps more like today's Grand Canyon as older Grand Canyon-age rock layers are revealed beneath today's "featured" young layers.

Above: **A geologist climbs a slope** of Entrada Sandstone in Rock Creek Canyon. Holes have developed in the rock face wherever the rock is poorly cemented. The Entrada Sandstone is about 160 million years old and is composed mostly of wind-deposited sands.

Right: **Two hikers stand near massive** "weathering pits" developed in the Entrada Sandstone near Cookie Jar Butte. The complete story of weathering-pit formation is not fully understood. The pits usually develop on windy ridgelines where narrow columns of disturbed, softer rock are exploited by the degenerative effects of water gathered in soft rock basins. During windy weather, whirling clouds of grit drill the depressions still deeper.

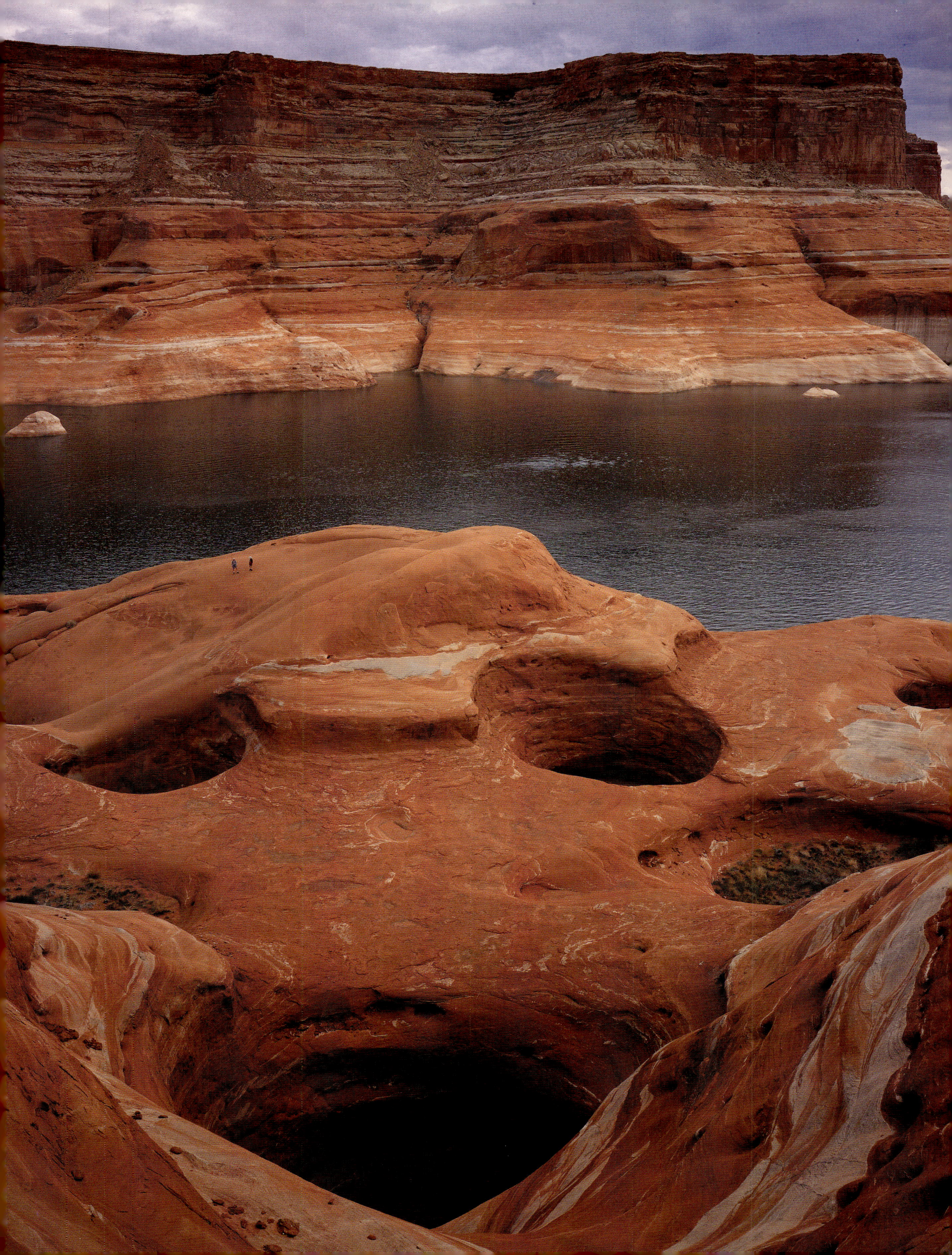

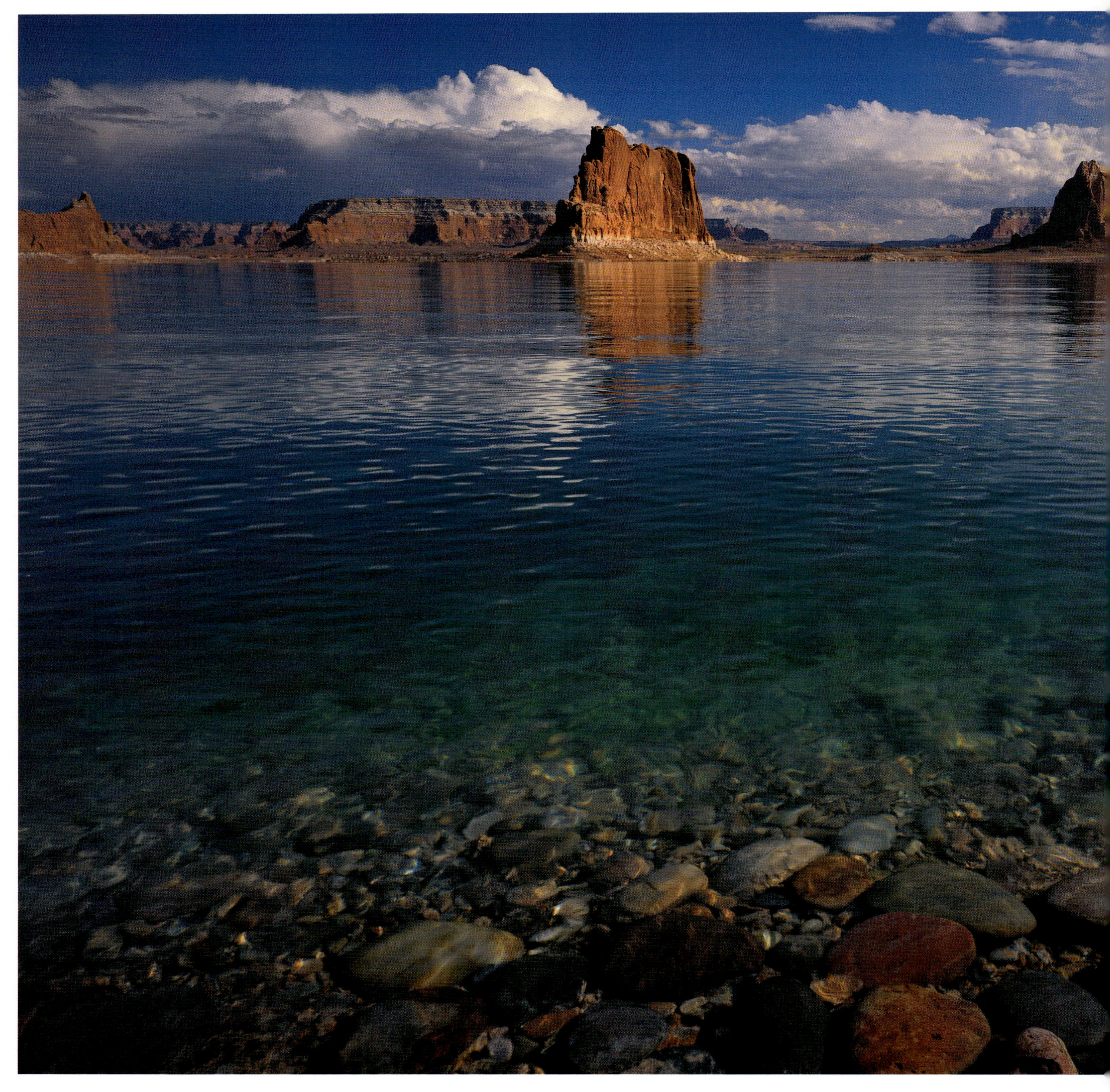

**Padre Bay is the largest bay** on Lake Powell. The name honors Francisco Dominguez and Silvestre Escalante, two Franciscan priests who crossed the Colorado River using an ancient Indian ford that now lies beneath today's Padre Bay. This first party of whites to see Glen Canyon on November 7, 1776, was returning to Santa Fe after an aborted attempt to reach the Spanish settlements in Monterey, California.

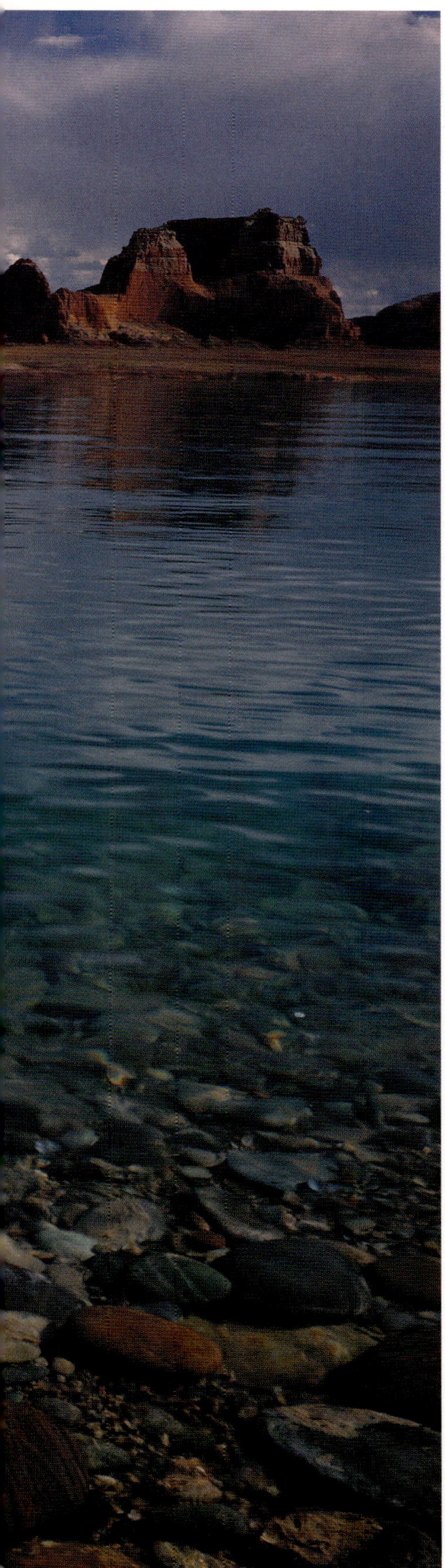

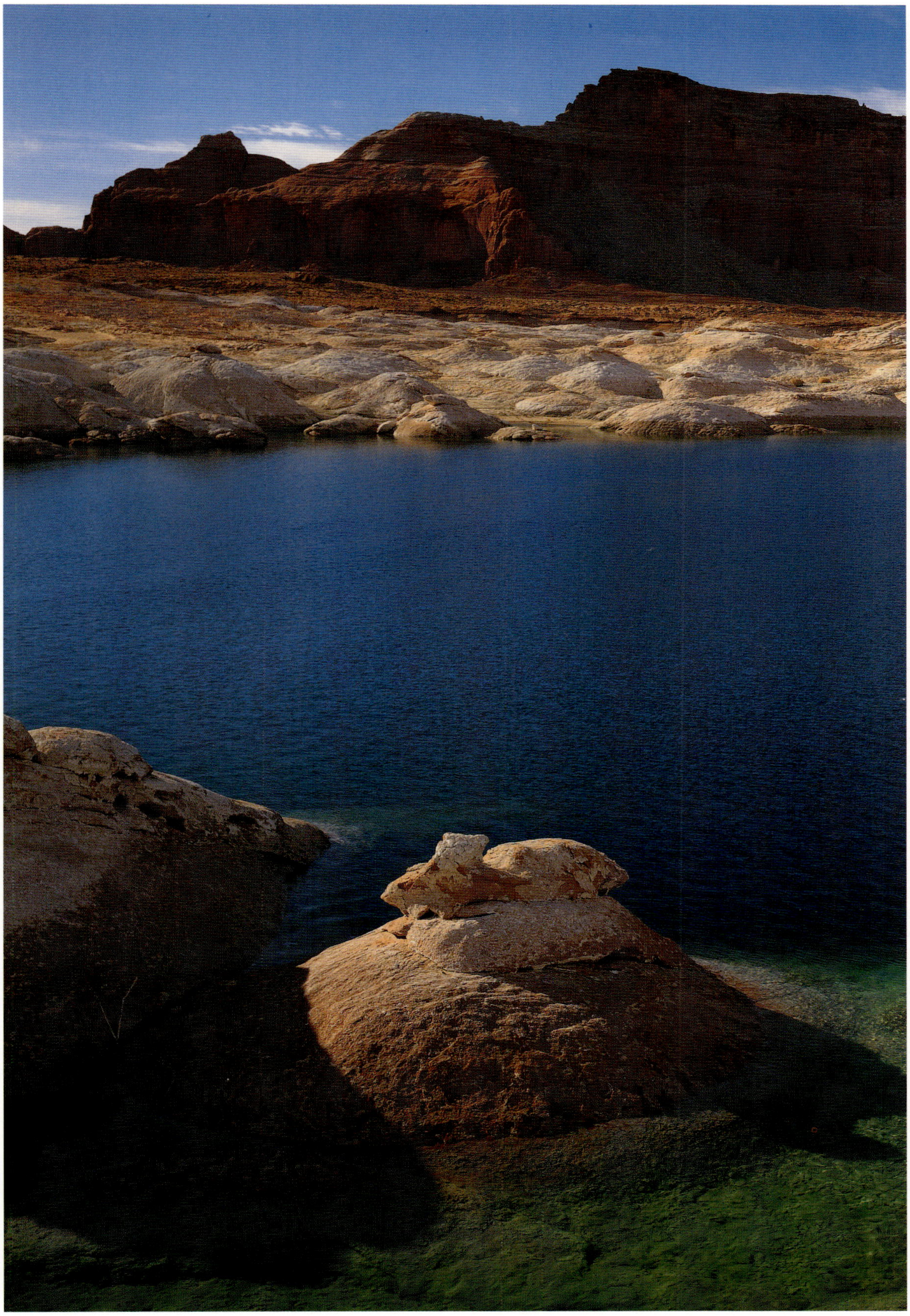

**Like many side canyons of Lake Powell,** Face Canyon's waters are sparkling clear for two reasons. Although both the main tributaries of Lake Powell—the Colorado River and the San Juan River—are famously muddy, they drop their sediment load where they enter the lake, leaving Lake Powell with mostly clear water. Also, naked rock shorelines assure that waves and boat wakes breaking at lake's edge don't muddy the waters. Under clear skies, deep waters appear blue and shallow waters look green.

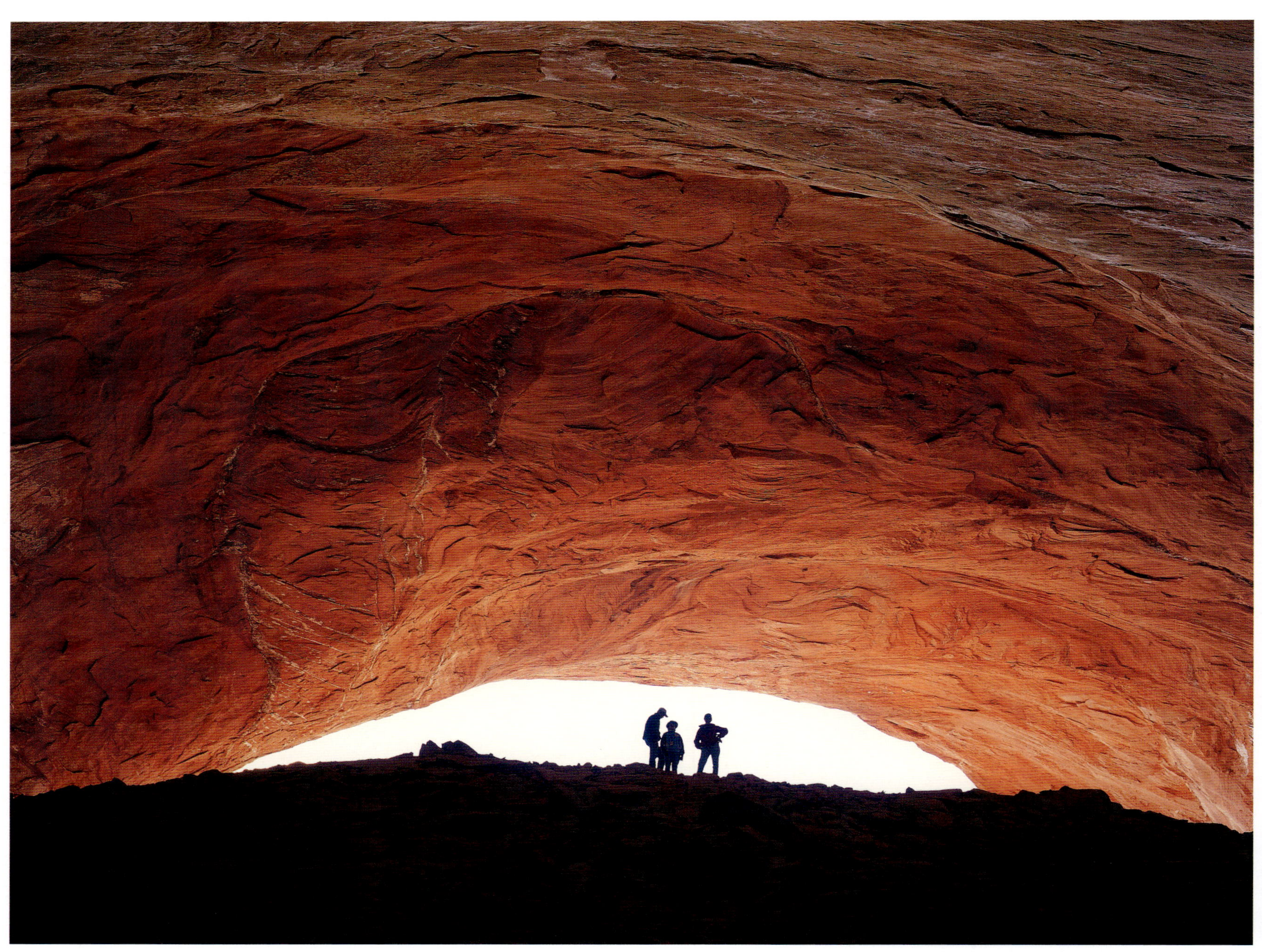

Above: **Hikers gather in a soaring stone alcove** in Fiftymile Canyon, a tributary of the Escalante Arm of Lake Powell. Sunlight ricochets upward from the sun-drenched entrance to bathe the alcove's vaulted ceiling in orange luminescence. An alcove's curved ceiling and hornlike entrance can act like a giant ear cocked toward the canyon beyond. Many times I've listened to the sounds of gurgling streams or spoken words emanating not from the canyon floor but from the roof of one of these grand sandstone grottoes.

Right: **Draperies of desert varnish** reach down cliffs of Navajo Sandstone in Iceberg Canyon. Desert varnish forms where ribbons of water flow down the faces of cliffs during rainy spells. The water leaves deposits of manganese and iron behind and supports an environment favorable to microorganisms, another common component of desert varnish. Navajo Sandstone is about 190 million years old. The source of its sands is surprising: It was carried by water and wind far from its origin in the then-young and rapidly eroding Appalachian Mountains.

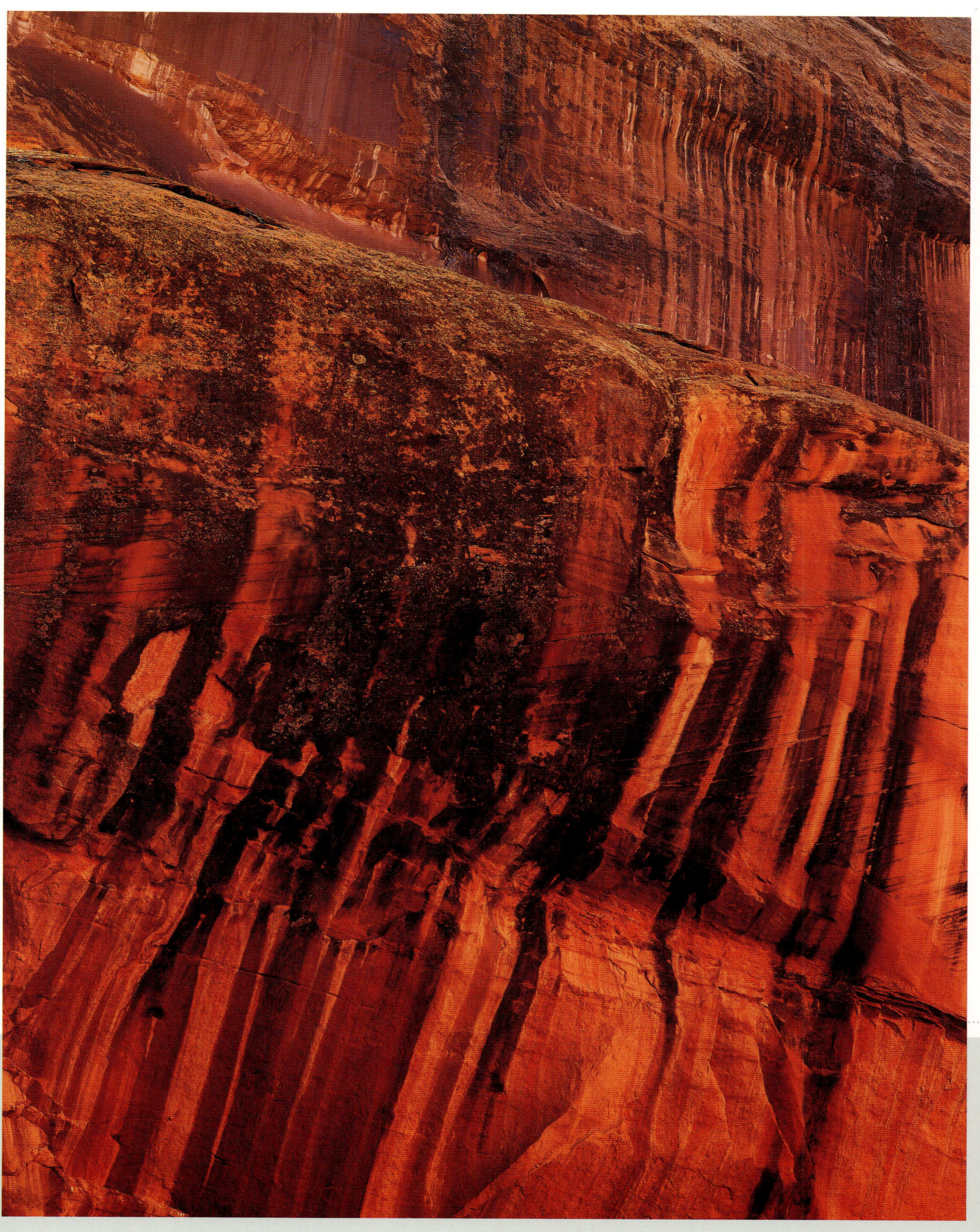

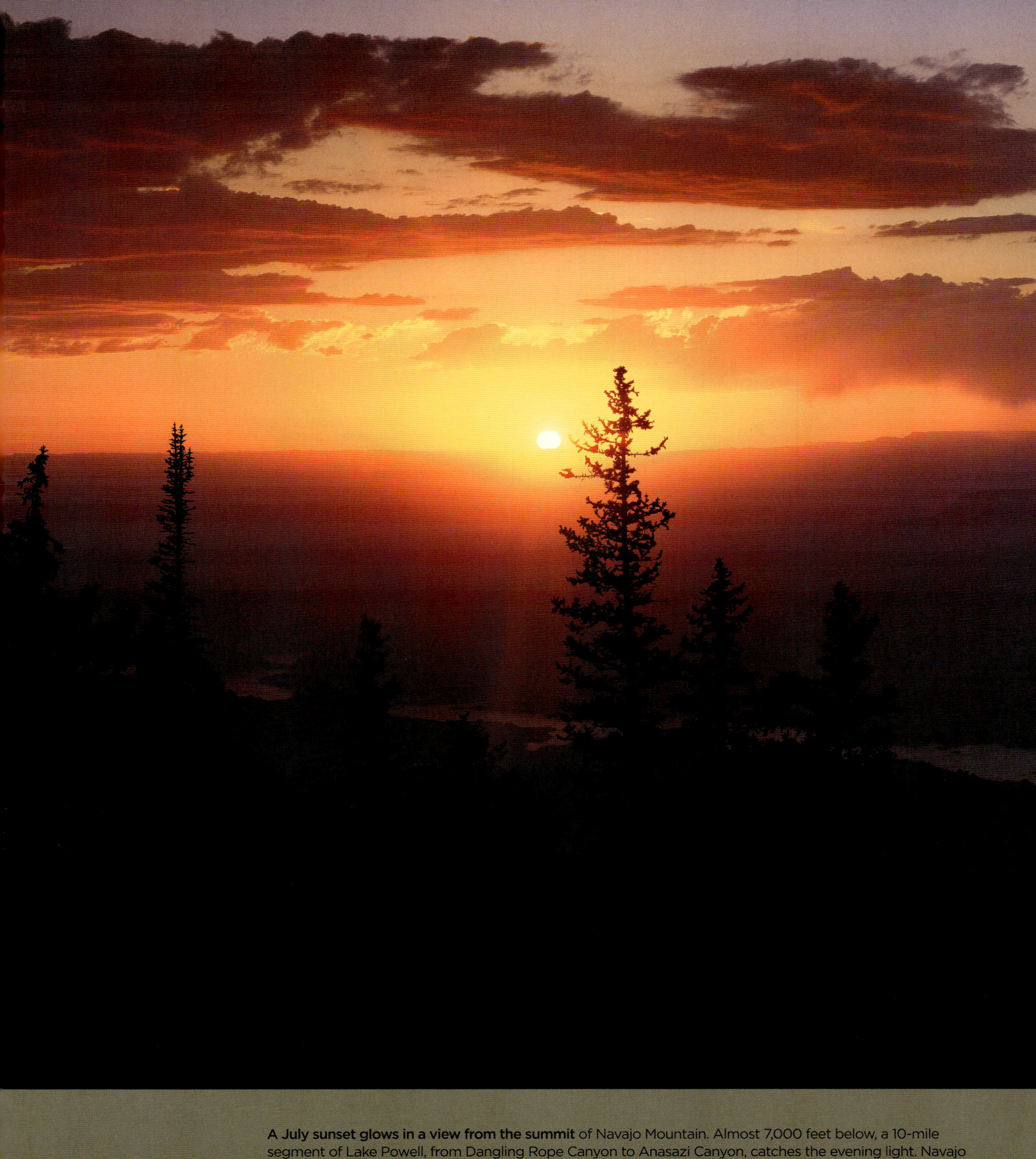

**A July sunset glows in a view from the summit** of Navajo Mountain. Almost 7,000 feet below, a 10-mile segment of Lake Powell, from Dangling Rope Canyon to Anasazi Canyon, catches the evening light. Navajo Mountain formed 30 to 40 million years ago when a mass of molten rock invaded to thrust up layer upon layer of sedimentary rocks. The 10,388-foot Navajo Mountain rises on the Navajo Nation.

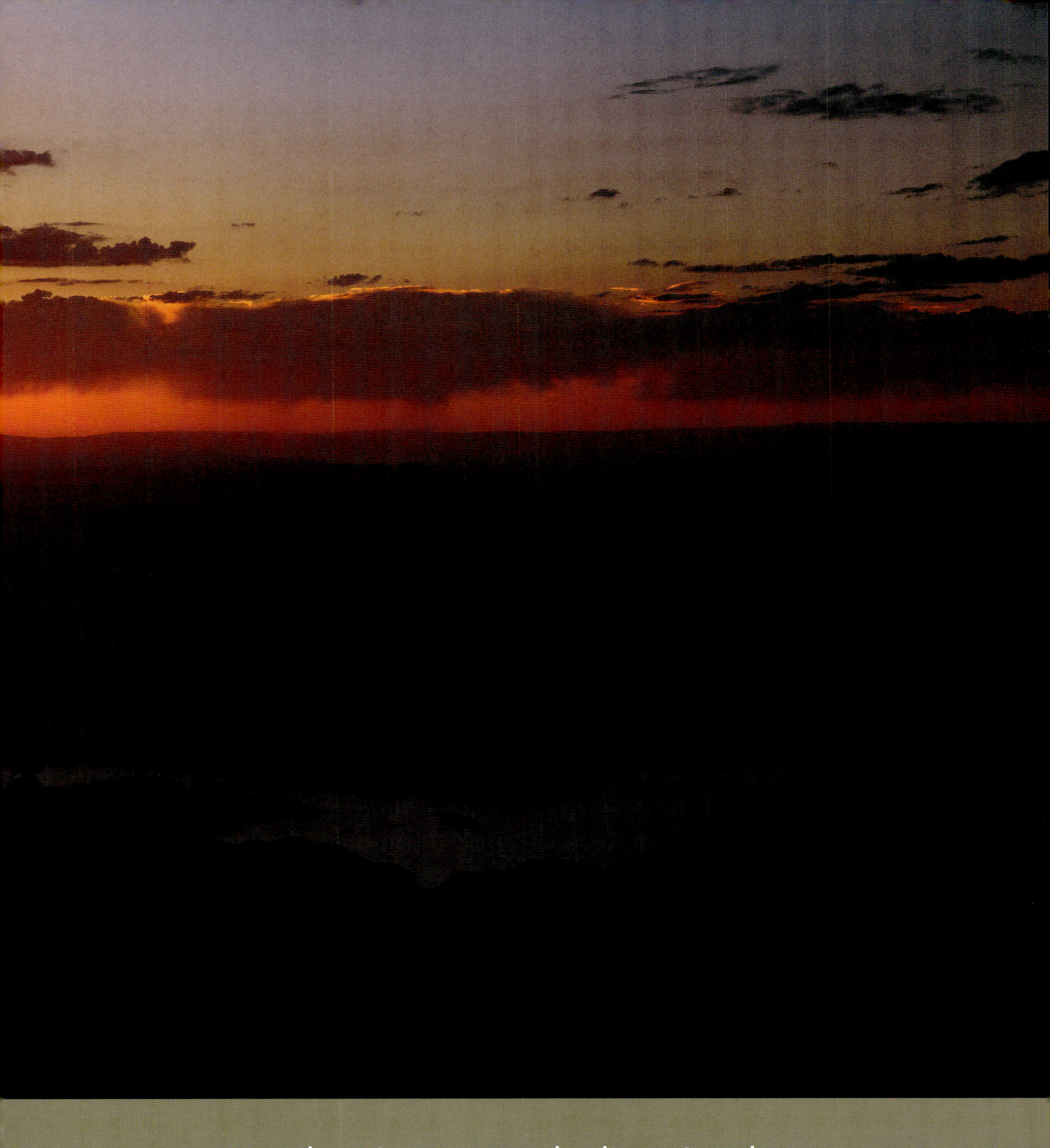

# THREE Lands Around the Lake

# THREE Lands Around the Lake

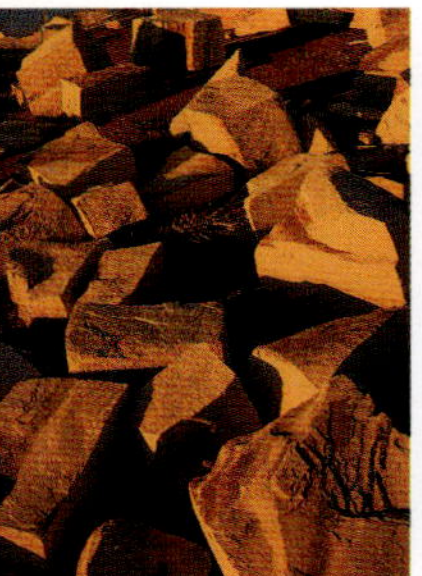
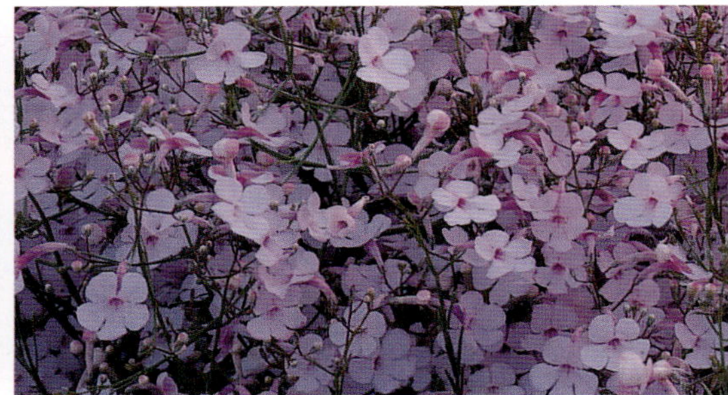
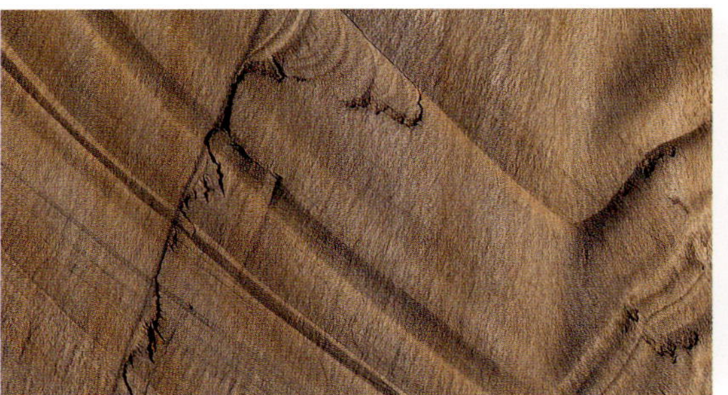
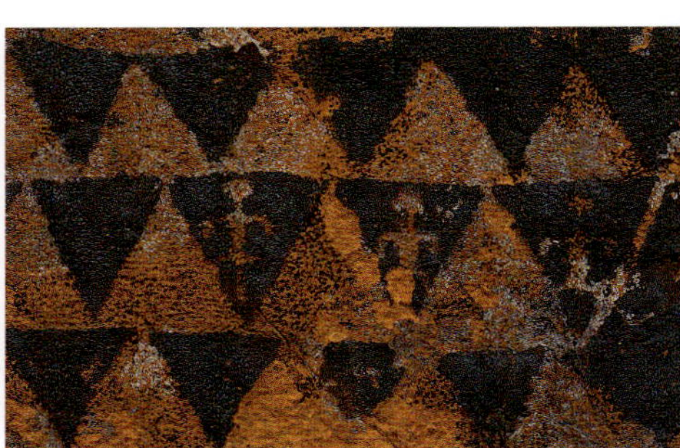

Twenty years ago, I joined a group of very determined slot canyon explorers. For two days we squeezed and waded through a sinuous slit in the rock called the Dark Arm, a remote and seldom-visited tributary of Lake Powell.

Parts of the Dark Arm were so narrow that an ordinary backpack was laughably impractical. Instead, we carried packs that were light and skinny. To keep the abrasive sandstone walls from grinding our elbows and knees to the bone, we wore medical wraps and pads. We carried ropes for use at drop-offs where we had to squirm down into what we called "rat holes" — places where the channel funneled downward through a confusion of boulders jammed between convoluted walls.

And, we carried headlamps for use in canyon sections where, even at noon, our route was too dark to see — the defile being just too deep, too narrow, and too twisting for sunlight to touch its floor.

At one location we came to what turned out to be the end of a false floor — a mass of boulders, cobbles, and rubble wedged between the walls (on which we were standing!) hanging above the true floor. We looked down into a dark chamber with walls so labyrinthine that we couldn't see the bottom. We dropped rocks to gauge the depth. Twenty-five feet. They plopped into water. We rappelled into a pool, waist deep, chest deep, and, finally, neck deep. Packs were lowered by rope and, for a short distance, we carried them balanced atop our heads, water up to our necks in the noontime night.

Finally, late on the second day, we broke out of the narrows, performed a final rappel, and established a last camp. The next morning we clambered up a rift to the rim.

Except for the last few miles, none of our route was visible from above–including views afforded by satellites and aircraft. Who would guess this improbable "cryptoscape" lies within the lands beyond the lake?

Left to right: **A jumble of angular sandstone** blocks rests near Dominguez Butte.
**Bush penstemon** blooms in June near Horseshoe Bend.
**A pattern of conchoidal fractures** graces a Navajo Sandstone cliff in Escalante Canyon.
**A geometric-patterned petroglyph** was pecked by Ancestral Puebloans nearly a thousand years ago.

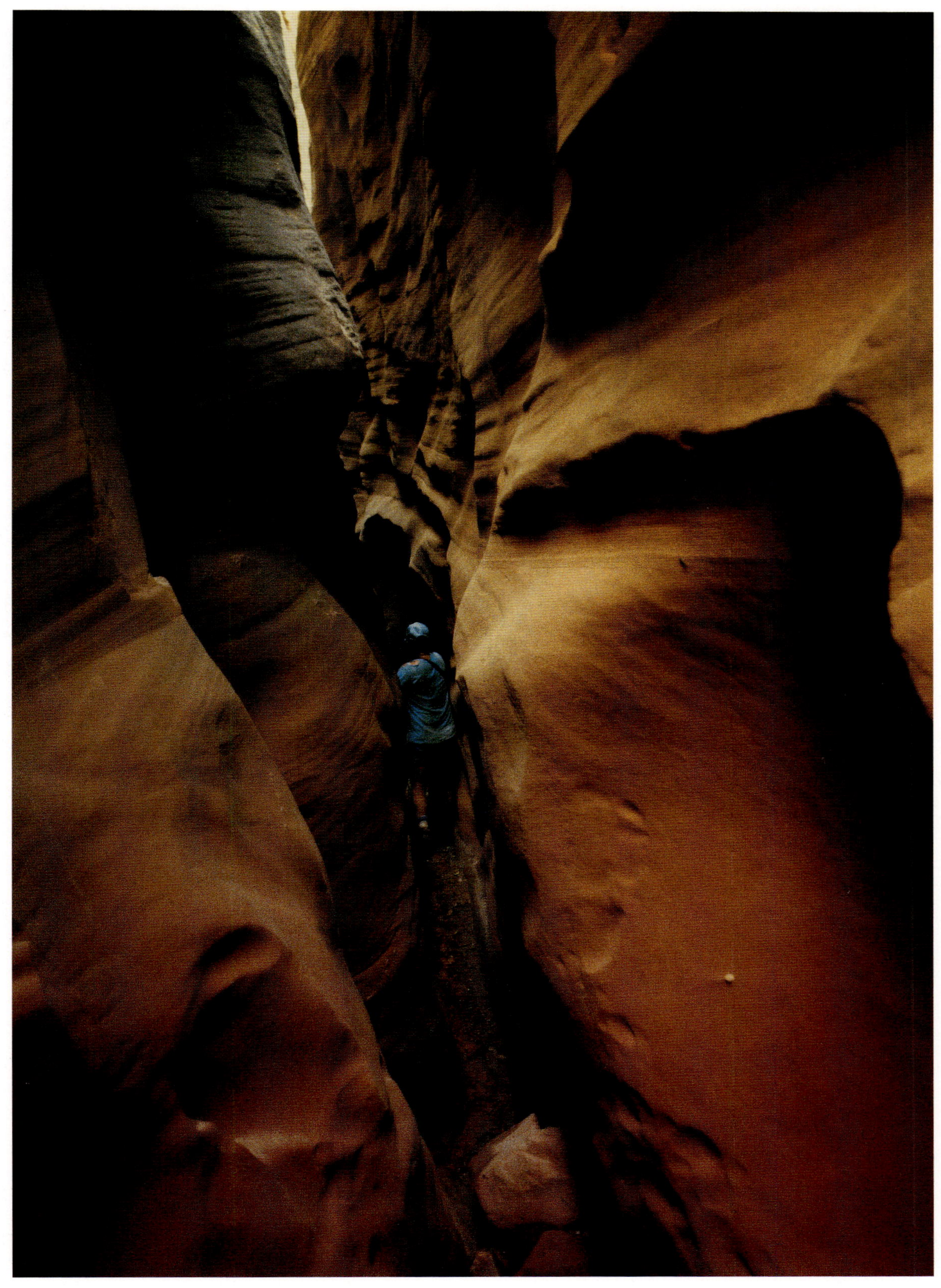

**A hiker fights his way through a slot** in the rock near Lake Powell. Slot canyons are wonderfully carved, fascinating, challenging, and dangerous. Flash floods originating miles away can inundate narrow canyons in seconds.

## What Is Beyond the Lake?

Although Glen Canyon National Recreation Area is chiefly known for Lake Powell, the lake actually covers little more than one-eighth of the park. The remaining area is the lake's polar opposite — desert and "wasteland," most of which is de facto wilderness.

Within view of the lake are expansive bench-lands distorted by columns of rising heat. Mesas, buttes, and spires populate portions of the flats while slickrock canyons, sometimes inhabited by chatty streamlets, crouch in the gulches between the mesas. There are enough slot canyons here to drive obsessive photographers crazy, and more than enough natural bridges, arches and alcoves, domes, and declivities to drive a mapmaker mad.

I sometimes think Lake Powell is no more than a clever distraction from the recreation area's most important feature: parched lands with rock monuments basking in the sun surrounded by skulking chasms. There's so much beyond the lake that the most appropriate answer to the question, "What's beyond the lake?" could be, "What lake?"

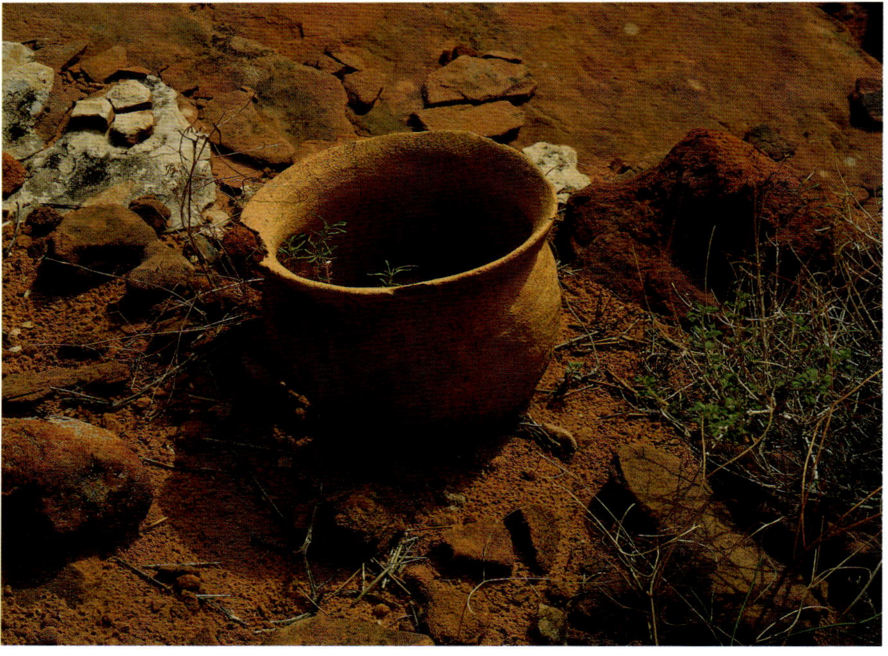

Glen Canyon National Recreation Area spreads far beyond the shores of Lake Powell into areas that are often assumed to be adjacent parks. The west rim of Marble Canyon, from Lee's Ferry to Navajo Bridge, is reasonably believed to be part of Grand Canyon National Park. Wrong. Large sections of the Escalante River area are commonly mistaken as Grand Staircase-Escalante National Monument lands. Wrong. The Orange Cliffs obviously belong to Canyonlands National Park. Wrong again. All are part of the Glen Canyon National Recreation Area beyond Lake Powell.

On the other hand, the Navajo Nation, whose northern boundary shadows the southern shore of Lake Powell, includes canyons and mesas that one might be forgiven for labeling as recreation-area territory. These include some of my favorite hideaways: West Canyon, upper Labyrinth Canyon, Anasazi Canyon, and Forbidding Canyon.

## Other Parks

When visitors boat in Glen Canyon National Recreation Area, they're surrounded not only by Glen Canyon's landscape treasures but by a complex of terrains assigned to and protected within other parks. Glen Canyon National Recreation Area shares borders with Grand Canyon National Park, Vermilion Cliffs National Monument, Grand Staircase-Escalante National Monument, Capitol Reef National Park, Canyonlands National Park, Dark Canyon Primitive Area, Grand Gulch Primitive Area, Antelope Canyon Navajo Tribal Park, and, of course, Rainbow Bridge National Monument — an impressive portfolio of great places.

Lake Powell lies at the heart of Glen Canyon National Recreation Area, and the recreation area is the hub of a wonderful assortment of Southwestern landscape jewels.

When the Great Creator — that's the Colorado River system — designed Glen Canyon and all that surrounds it, it fashioned a sensationally lovely landscape ensemble. Glen Canyon and its surroundings are all part of a territory of extreme visual drama.

**I have never found an Ancestral Puebloan pot,** but some of my friends have been more fortunate. This one, unfortunately, was probably stolen by a looter. The Ancestral Puebloans and their predecessors roamed Glen Canyon for a thousand years or more. Today's Hopi Indians and the pueblo tribes of the Southwest probably descended from the Ancestral Puebloans, who likely abandoned Glen Canyon when a lengthy drought made farming all but impossible.

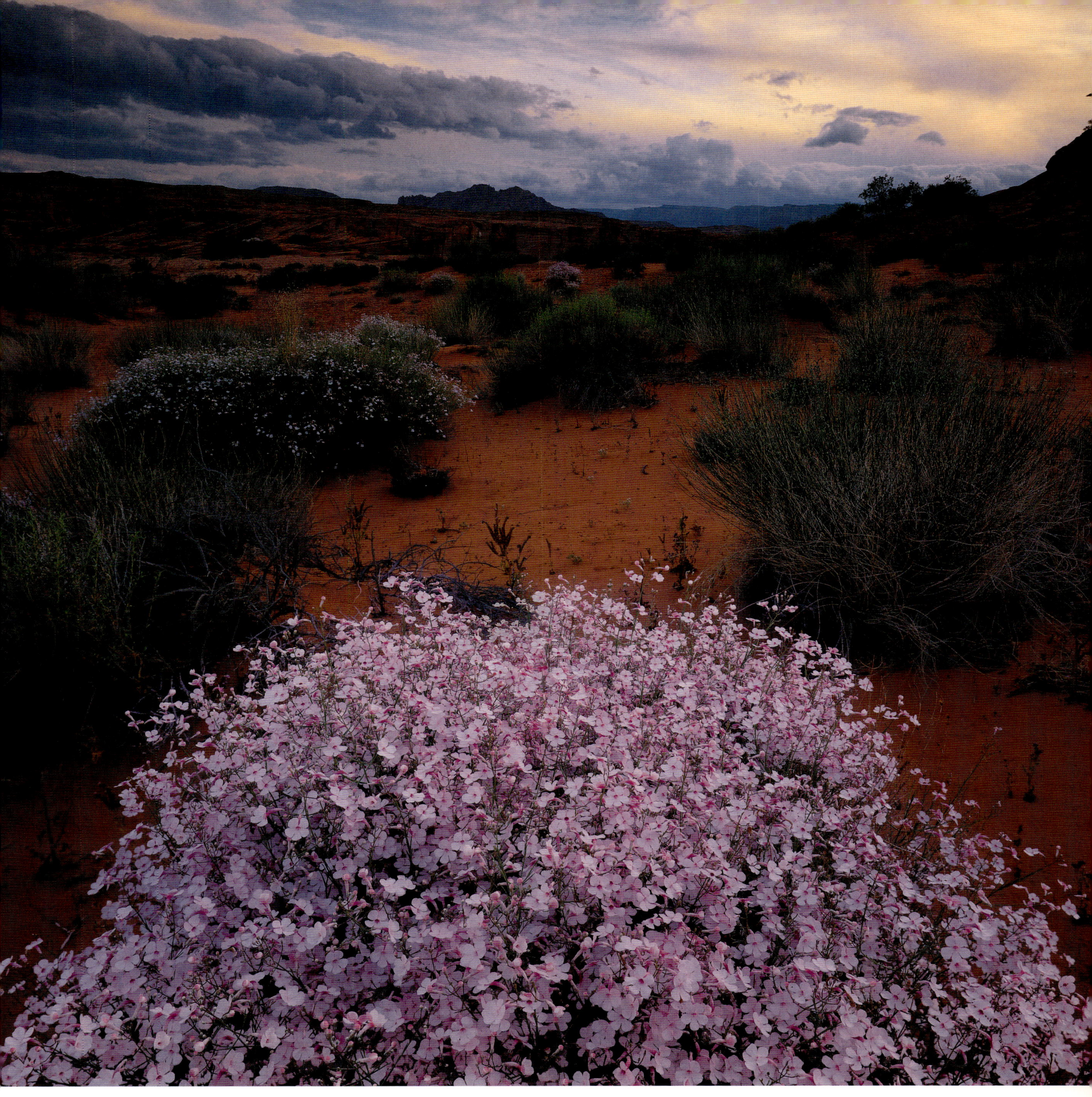

**Bush penstemon blooms** in late spring and early summer. Its purple flowers brighten sandy areas otherwise dominated by blackbrush and blue sage.

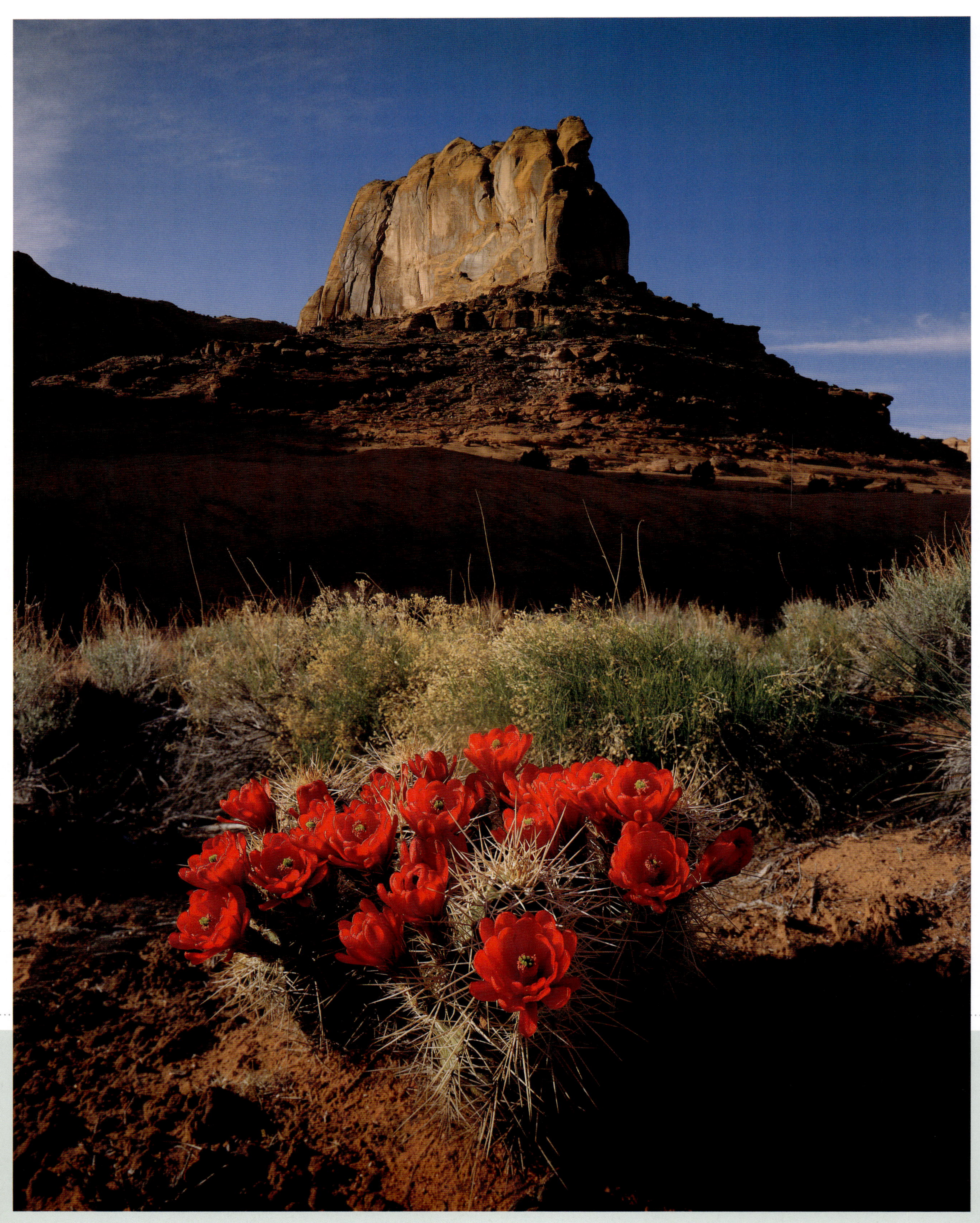

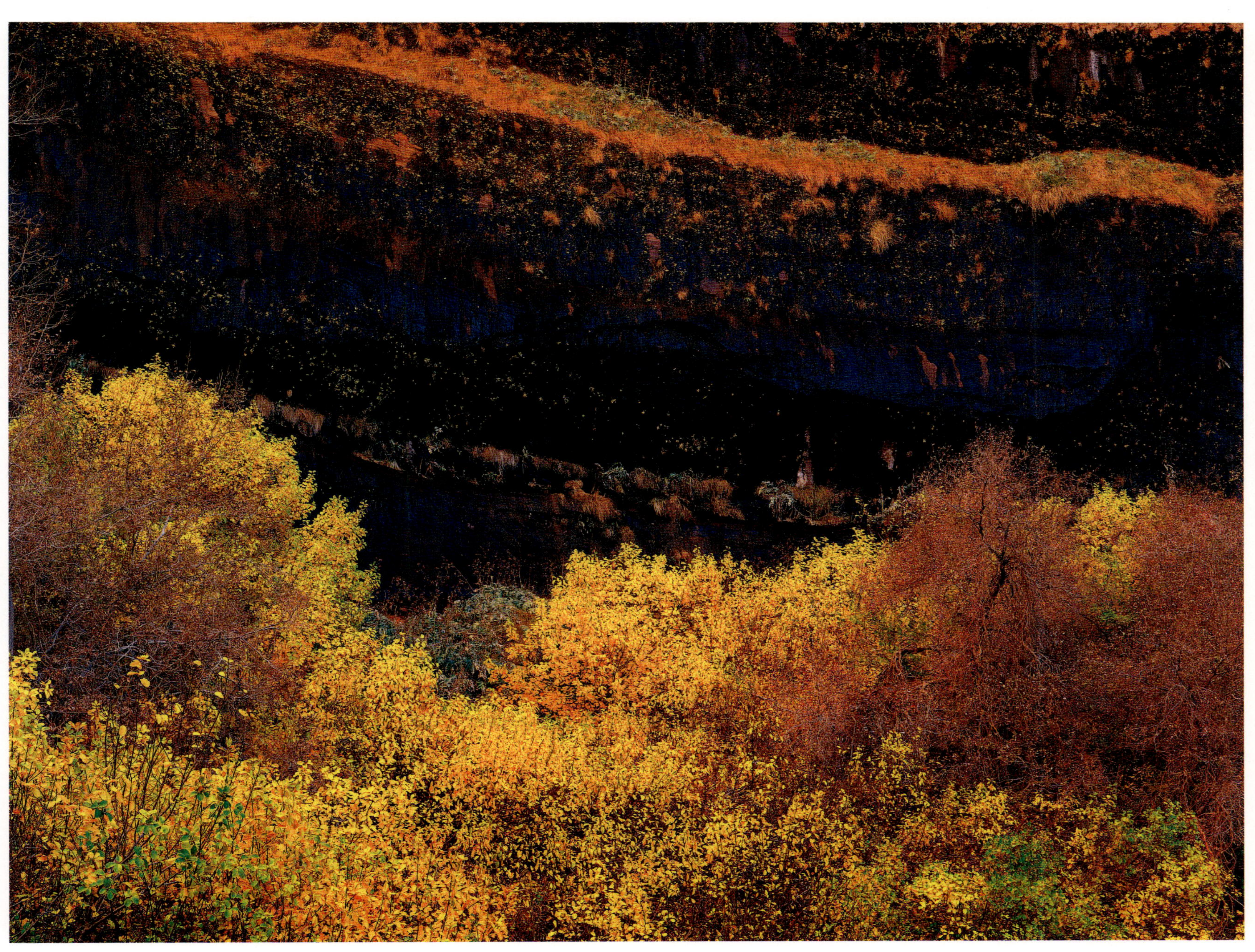

Left: **The bright blooms of a claretcup hedgehog cactus** glow in the light of an April afternoon in Stevens Canyon, a tributary of Escalante Canyon. Those sections of Escalante Canyon and its tributaries that are beyond the reach of Lake Powell are perhaps the most glittering backcountry jewels in all of Glen Canyon National Recreation Area.

Above: **In early December, the final fall colors** brighten a curving amphitheater wall at the upper end of Explorer Canyon. Spring waters seeping out of the sandstone dampen the cliffs and feed an oasis of pools and vegetation at the base of the cliffs.

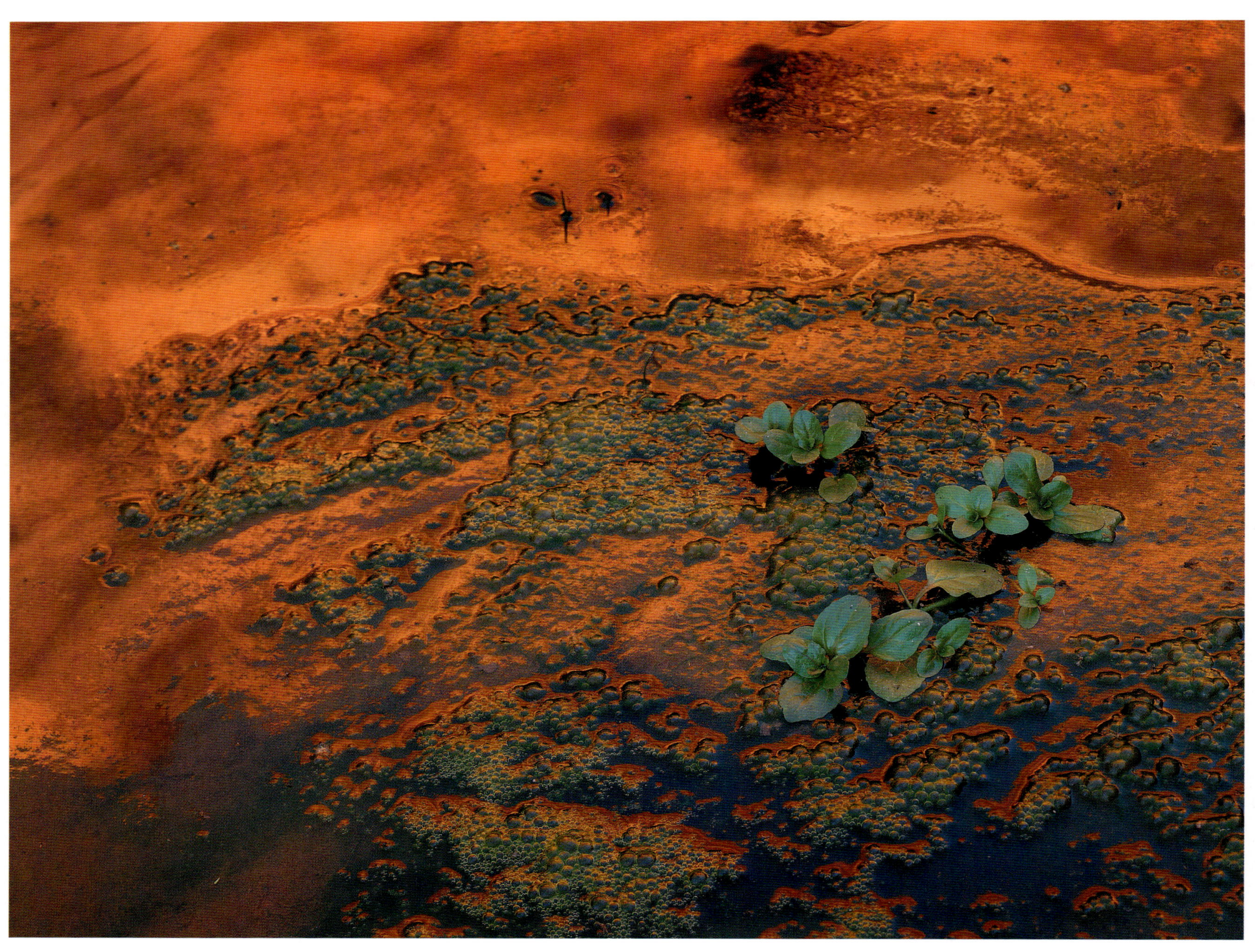

Above: **Algae thrives in a shallow pool** in a nameless tributary of the Escalante Arm of Lake Powell. The reflection of a sunlit cliff paints the waters gold on a November afternoon.

Right: **Just where Lake Powell at its highest levels** comes to an end in West Canyon, flash floods have sculpted a hauntingly beautiful corridor from Navajo Sandstone. I was once wading through this canyon's pools when several bushel baskets of sand suddenly plopped from above into the water immediately behind me. The crash made me jump, and I was a little edgy for the rest of the afternoon.

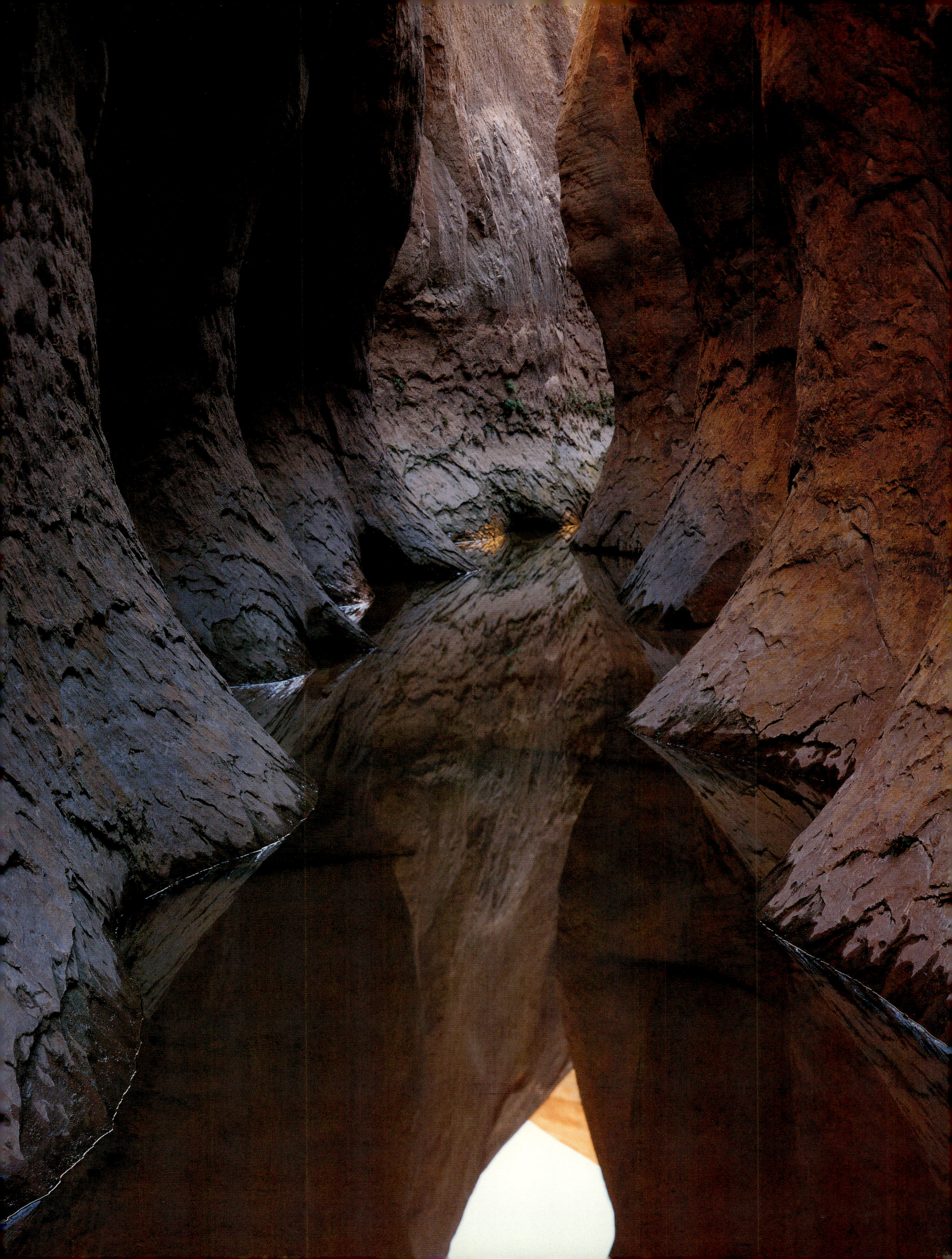

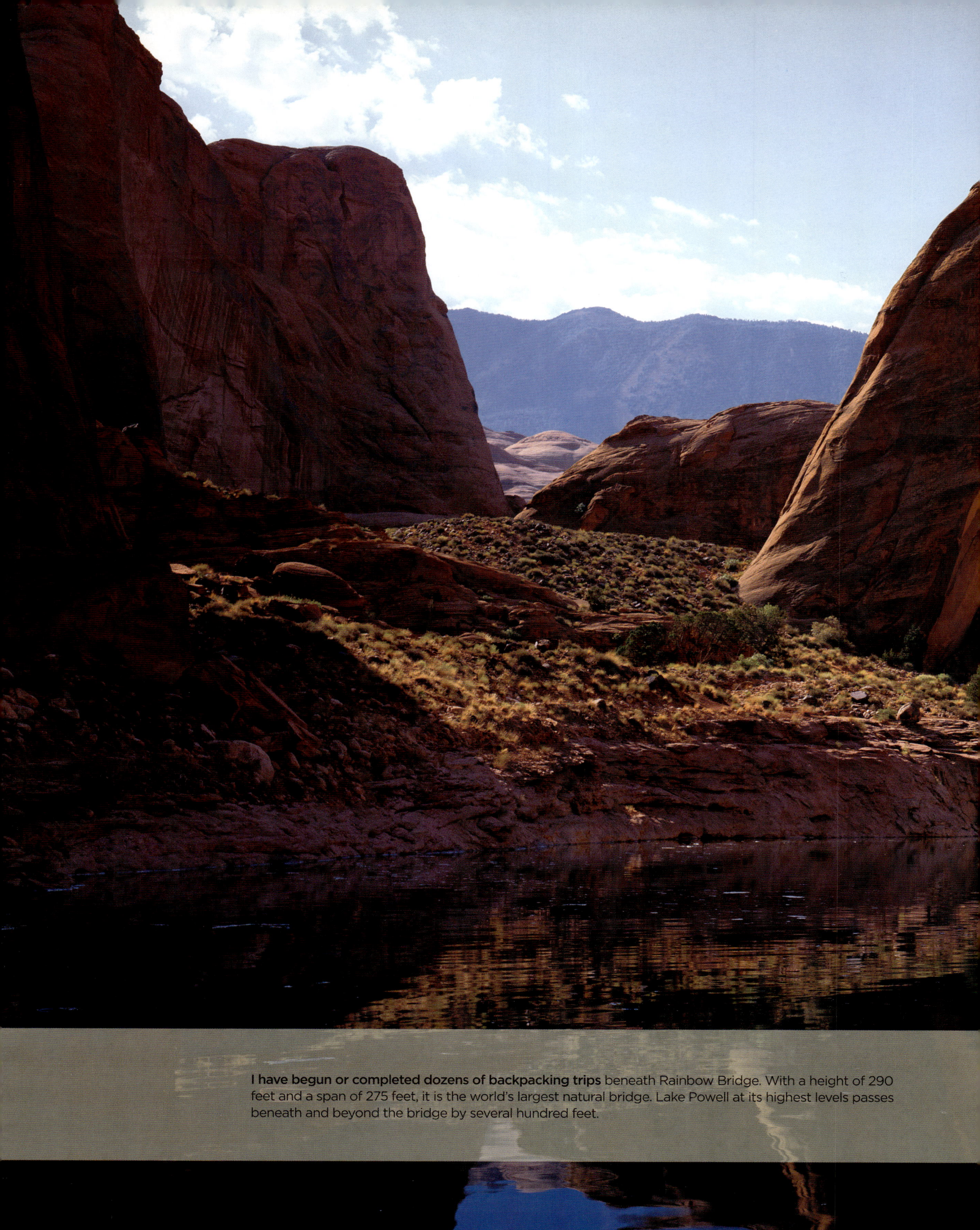

**I have begun or completed dozens of backpacking trips** beneath Rainbow Bridge. With a height of 290 feet and a span of 275 feet, it is the world's largest natural bridge. Lake Powell at its highest levels passes beneath and beyond the bridge by several hundred feet.

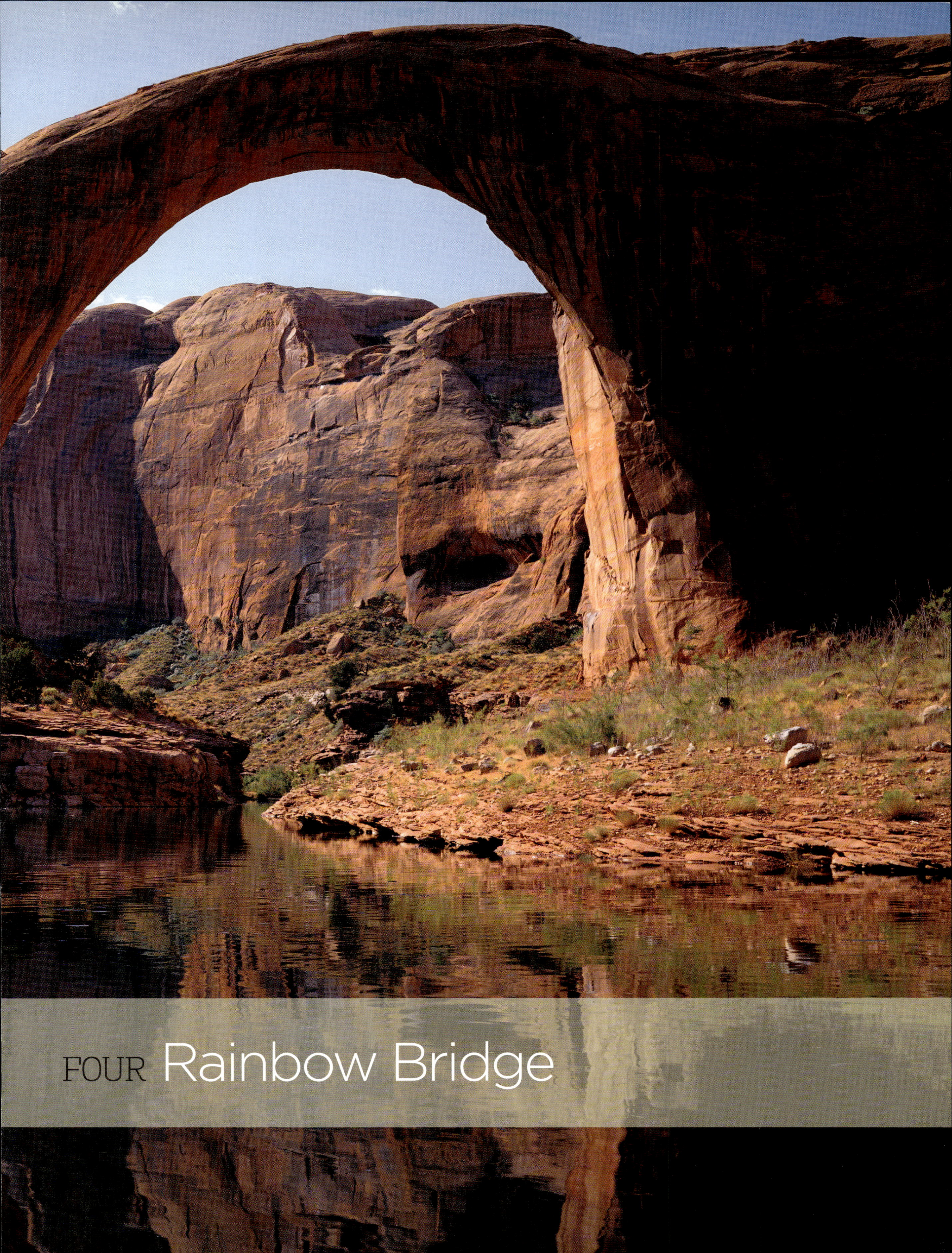

# FOUR Rainbow Bridge

# FOUR Rainbow Bridge

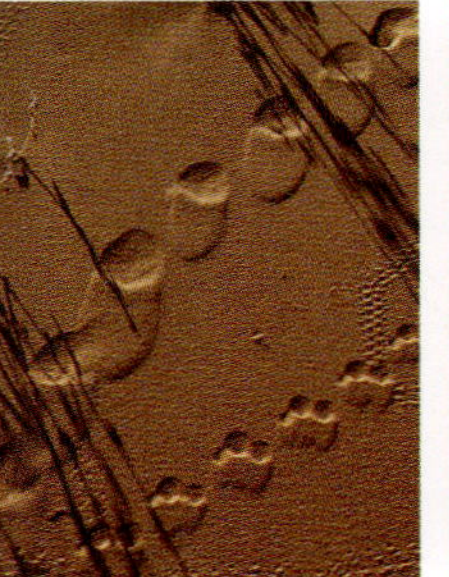
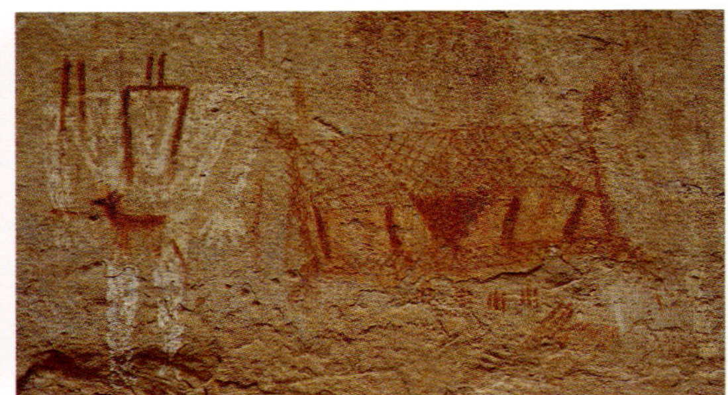
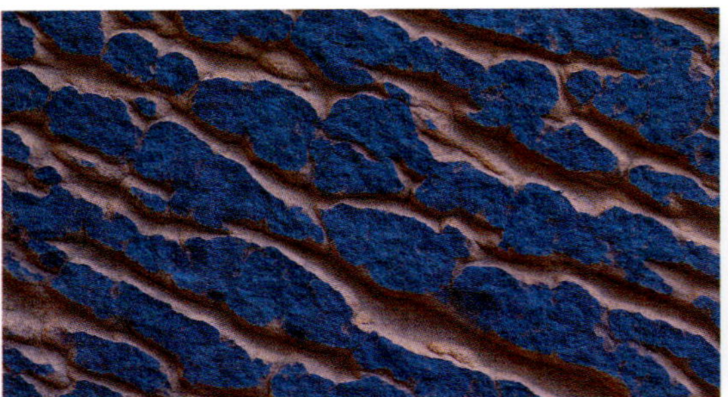
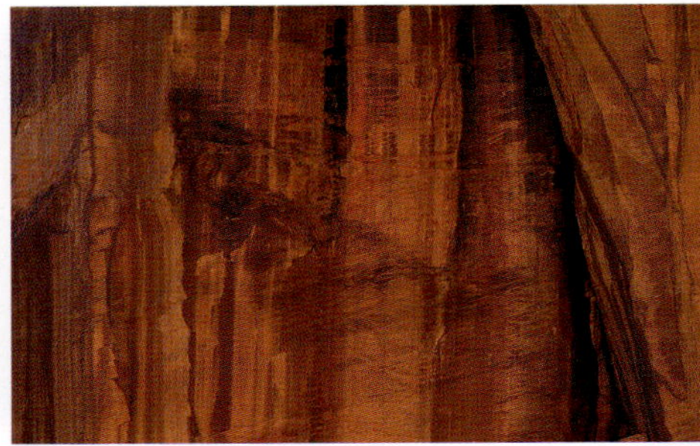

Soon after moving to Page, Arizona, at the edge of Glen Canyon National Recreation Area, I experienced an epiphany: Rainbow Bridge was located in *my* backyard. So, naturally, some friends and I began making plans to explore the farthest reaches of my new property.

In the spring of 1982, we stepped out of my apartment, locked the door, hefted our backpacks and started walking east toward the back forty. In front of us lay a maze of topographic obstacles — canyons, slots, mesas, and stinking desert — but during the next week and a half we surmounted them all.

The backpack trip crystallized into an epic that still arises in conversations 30 years later. It included one twilight therapy session in West Canyon when the six of us gathered around an evening primrose and for an hour watched as one bloom nearly imperceptibly but resolutely opened in the fading light. It was a once-in-a-lifetime visual opus witnessed exclusively by a little group of sandstone pilgrims.

We walked in beauty, challenge, wonder, and, on one occasion, great drama as an angry flash flood swept past our canyon camp. On the morning of the tenth day, we turned a canyon corner and first glimpsed the great span in my backyard, Rainbow Bridge.

Left to right: **Insect tracks** dot the sands of Face Canyon.
**Ancestral Puebloans** created this pictograph in Cliff Canyon.
**The eroding surface** of a Navajo Sandstone boulder near Ribbon Canyon is shown in detail.
**Streaks of desert varnish** decorate Rainbow Bridge.

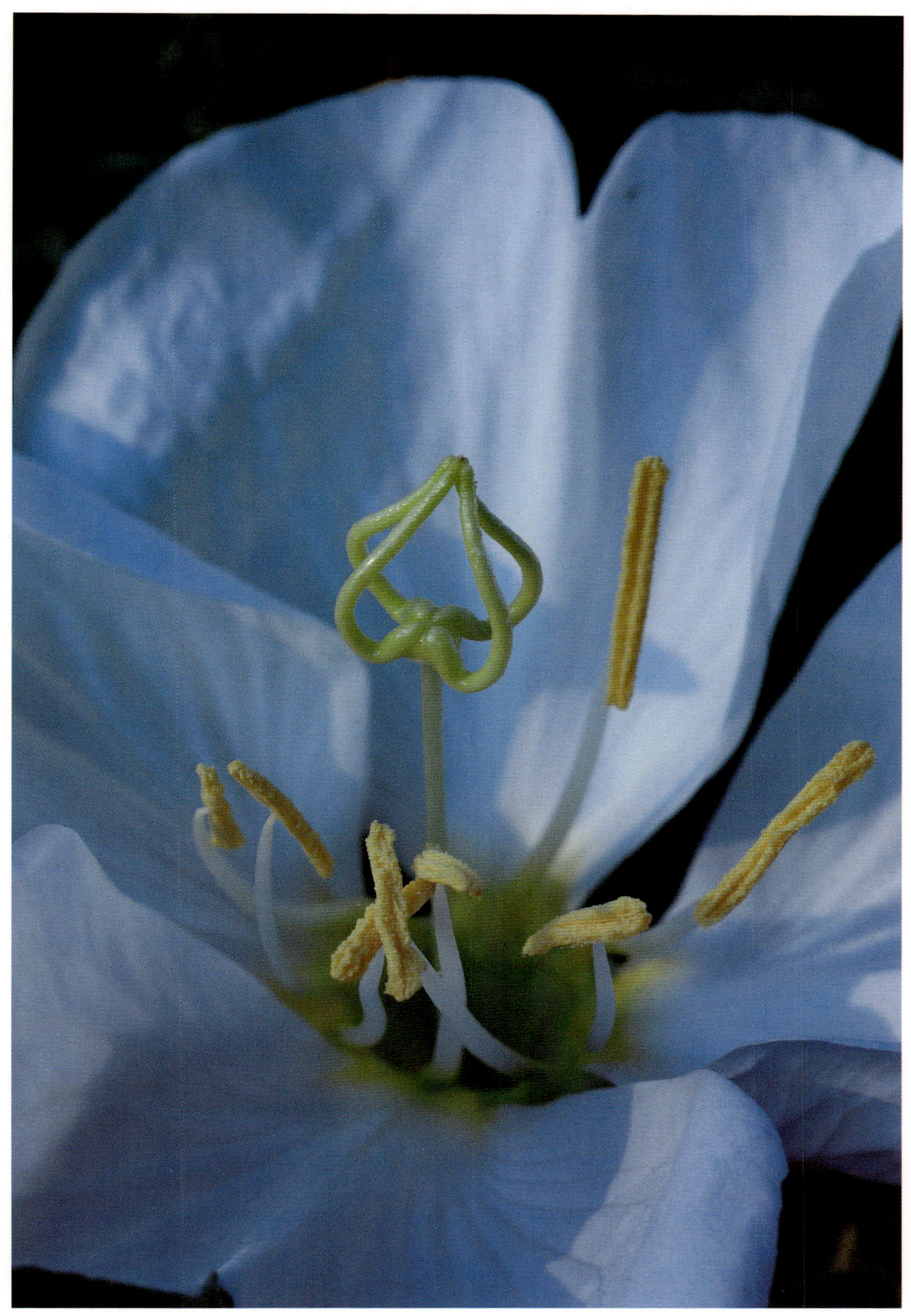

**An evening primrose blooms** near Fiftymile Point in late April.

## Discovery

In the first years of the 20th century, Rainbow Bridge remained hidden in a network of canyons and cracks sequestered in a remote region of what had just become the state of Utah.

It was officially "discovered" in August 1909 when two groups, one led by archaeologist Byron Cummings along with explorer John Wetherill, and another led by General Land Office surveyor William Douglass, joined forces to find the bridge together.

Both groups, of course, employed Native American guides. And yet, both groups recognized only *their* Indian guide as the one who *really* knew the way. And both groups later insisted that it was the other expedition that attached itself to theirs. Even today it's not exactly clear who was leading and who was hustling to avoid being scooped. (Most locals think the camp follower was Mr. Douglass.)

These men, however, were probably not the first Anglos to come upon the bridge. Prospectors had been scrambling across the mesas and through these canyons since at least the 1880s. Some of them left inscriptions in nearby canyons. They were looking for minerals, however, not marvels. Peculiar features were sprinkled everywhere in this sandstone bewilderment, and a big stone bridge was just another of them. So, the men didn't bother to sing out about the rainbow turned to stone.

Delving still deeper into time, we find plentiful archaeological evidence that the Ancestral Puebloans (formerly known as the Anasazi) lived in the vicinity of the bridge for centuries. And earlier Native American groups likely visited the bridge long before the Ancestral Puebloans.

Thus, we don't know who first saw Rainbow Bridge. The names and cultures have been lost in the sandstorms of time.

## The Geologic Story

By studying the canyon's details, we can intuit what transpired geologically to create Rainbow Bridge. We can see how Bridge Creek once meandered as it descended from the slopes of Navajo Mountain, swinging through a series of loops along the way. Over time, as the stream eroded downward, it also carved laterally, creating larger and larger loops until some of them intersected one another by breaking through their common walls. At the breakthrough points, the rock partitions almost always collapsed.

But not *quite* always. At the future site of Rainbow Bridge, Bridge Creek undercut an unusually high and solid fin of rock that held firm while the creek bored a hole through its foundations. Geologists calculate that this first pilot hole was drilled between 10,000 and 50,000 years ago. Since then, the little stream has carved still deeper into bedrock, while up above, slabs and sheets of rock have fallen from the underside of the span. This is why the free opening of Rainbow Bridge has grown with time. It has not always been the shape we admire today, and today's form will evolve into still others.

**Grasses, dominated by ricegrass,** thrive near Rainbow Bridge after a wet winter. Rainbow Bridge National Monument lies within Rainbow Bridge Canyon but includes only 160 acres. Upper Bridge Creek beyond the monument boundary lies on the Navajo Nation.

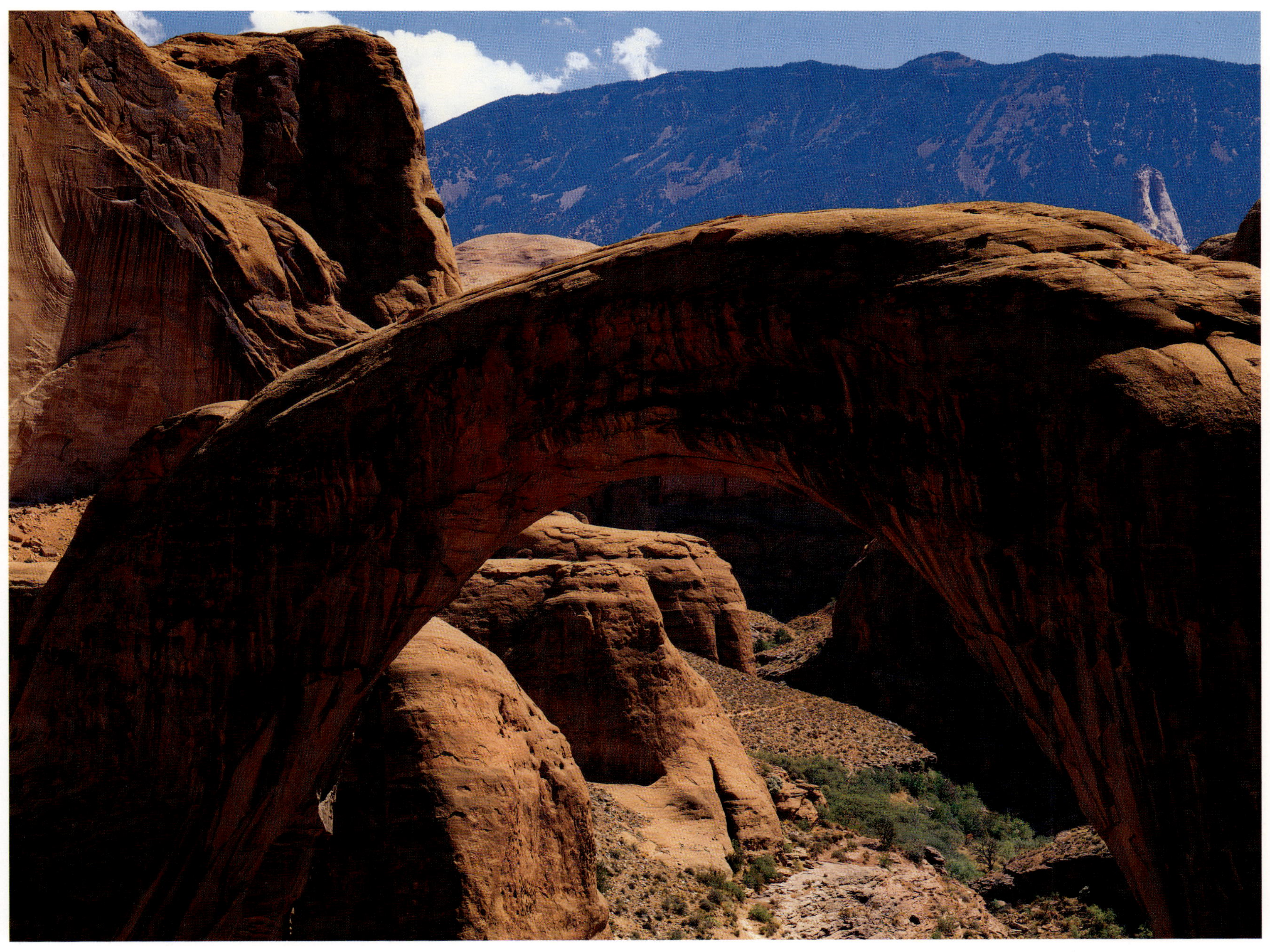

## The Future

Rainbow Bridge is composed of Navajo Sandstone, but it spans a narrow inner gorge carved from Kayenta Sandstone, a rock layer that is slightly older and more resistant to erosion. One important repercussion of the two-part composition is that the waters of Lake Powell can never reach or degrade the main span of the bridge. We do not know how long the bridge will stand. It could crumble next week or soar for many more millennia.

Many tens of thousands of visitors admire Rainbow Bridge every year. Most come by boat; some — perhaps a few dozen — follow one of two old trails to the bridge. It has been more than a hundred years since the bridge's documented discovery by non-Native Americans, but the satisfaction of coming upon a huge natural stone bridge seemingly lost in an endless canyon web still awaits those willing to invest some time and eat some trail dust.

**The summit of Navajo Mountain** stands 5.5 miles away and almost 7,000 feet above the base of Rainbow Bridge. The headwaters of Bridge Creek are located on the mountain's upper slopes.

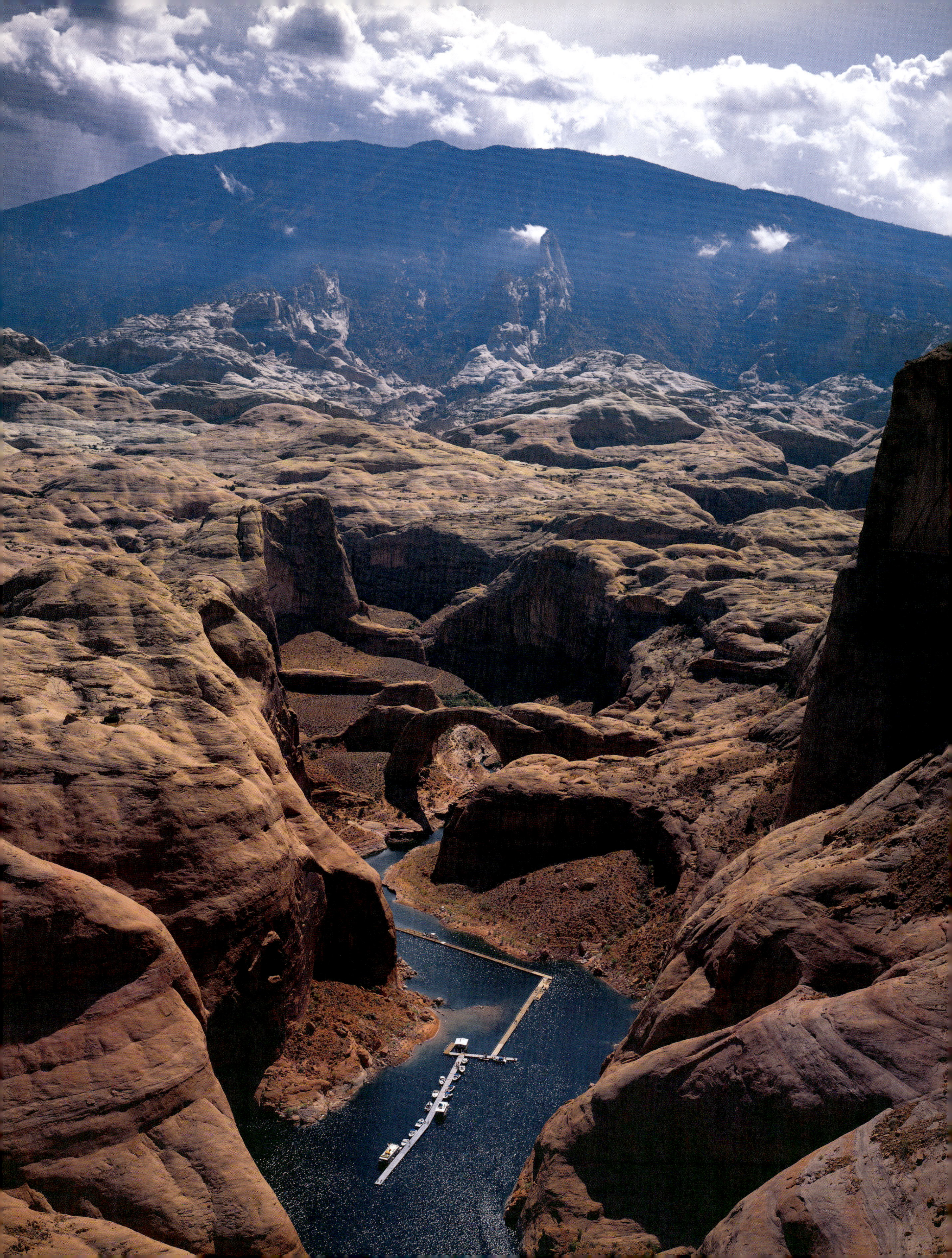

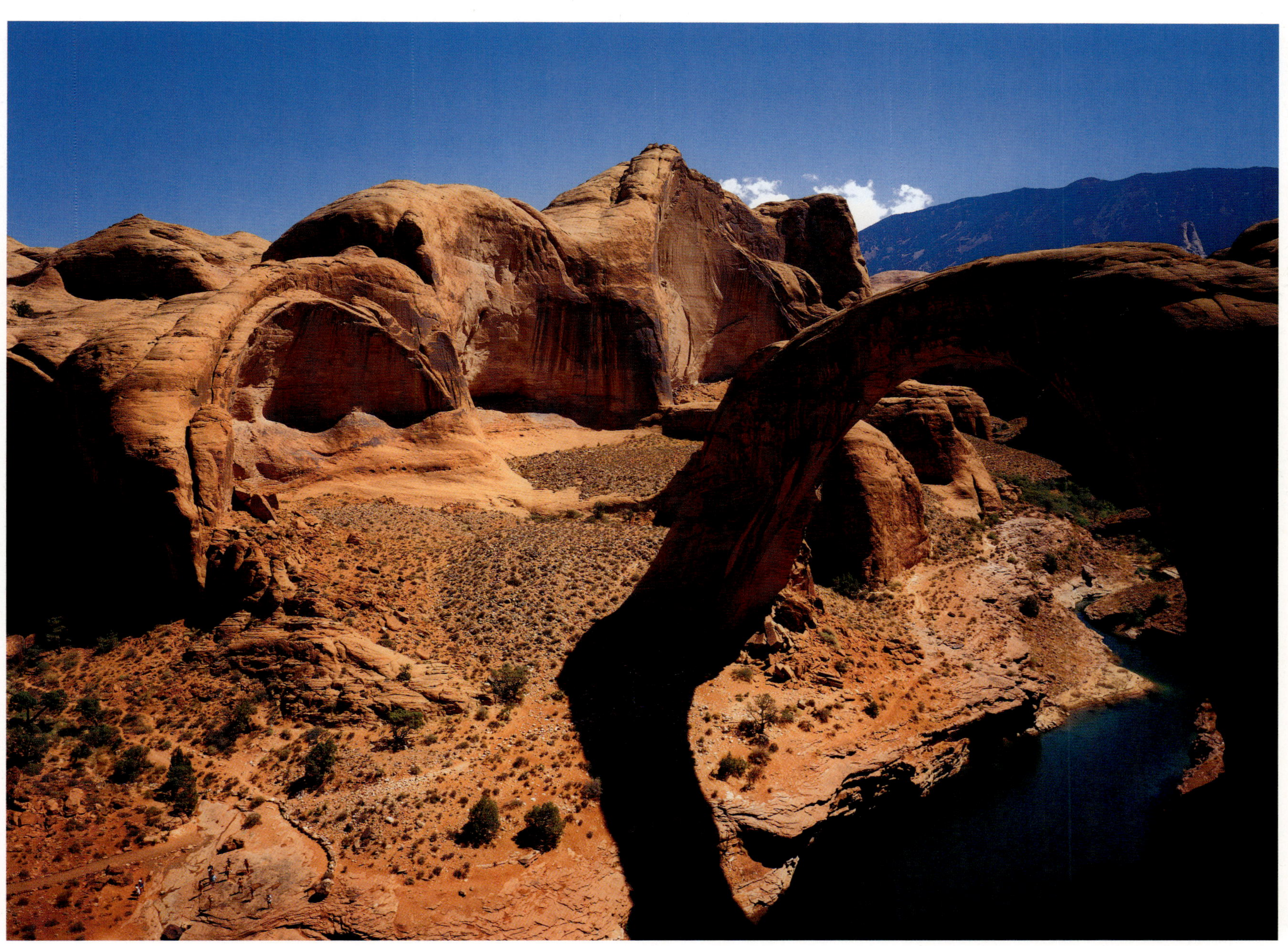

Left: **While Glen Canyon Dam** was under construction, plans were made to prevent Lake Powell from invading Rainbow Bridge National Monument, an ambition dictated by Congress. The project probably would have included two dams (one upstream and one downstream from the bridge), a tunnel to divert Bridge Creek into Forbidding Canyon, and a maze of access roads. Ultimately, however, because of a lack of funding and a shortage of time, the project was dropped.

Above: **Evidence of the events** and processes that created Rainbow Bridge is plentiful when the canyon's northeast wall is observed. Multiple alcoves carved by wide swings of younger Bridge Creek stand side by side, while knobs of rock rise like islands near the canyon's middle. The "islands" are remnants of the rock partitions that separated the meanders. (In this view they lie half hidden behind the left leg of the bridge.) Bridge Creek punched a shortcut hole through the base of an unusually tall and sturdy partition, beginning the carving of what evolved into Rainbow Bridge.

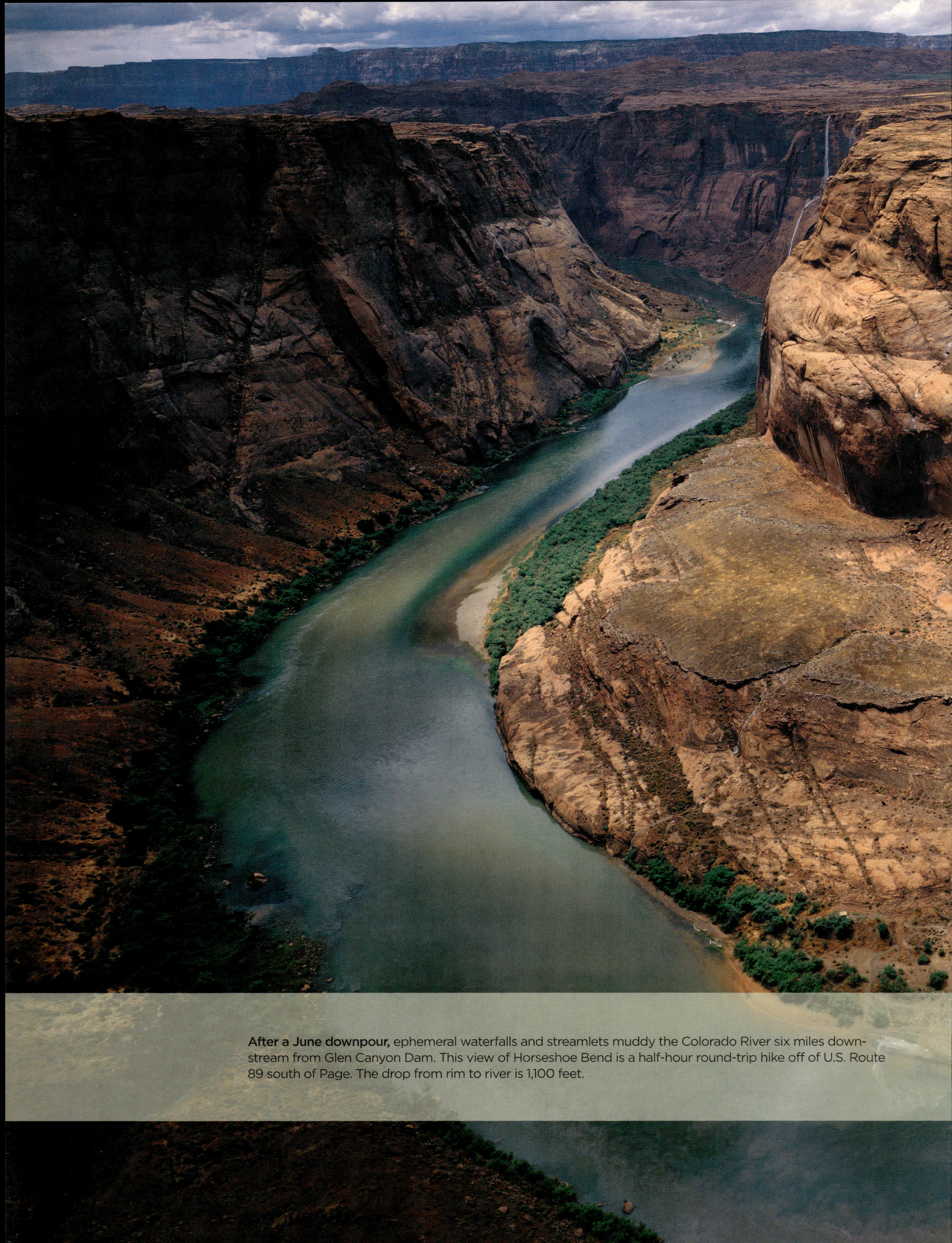

**After a June downpour,** ephemeral waterfalls and streamlets muddy the Colorado River six miles downstream from Glen Canyon Dam. This view of Horseshoe Bend is a half-hour round-trip hike off of U.S. Route 89 south of Page. The drop from rim to river is 1,100 feet.

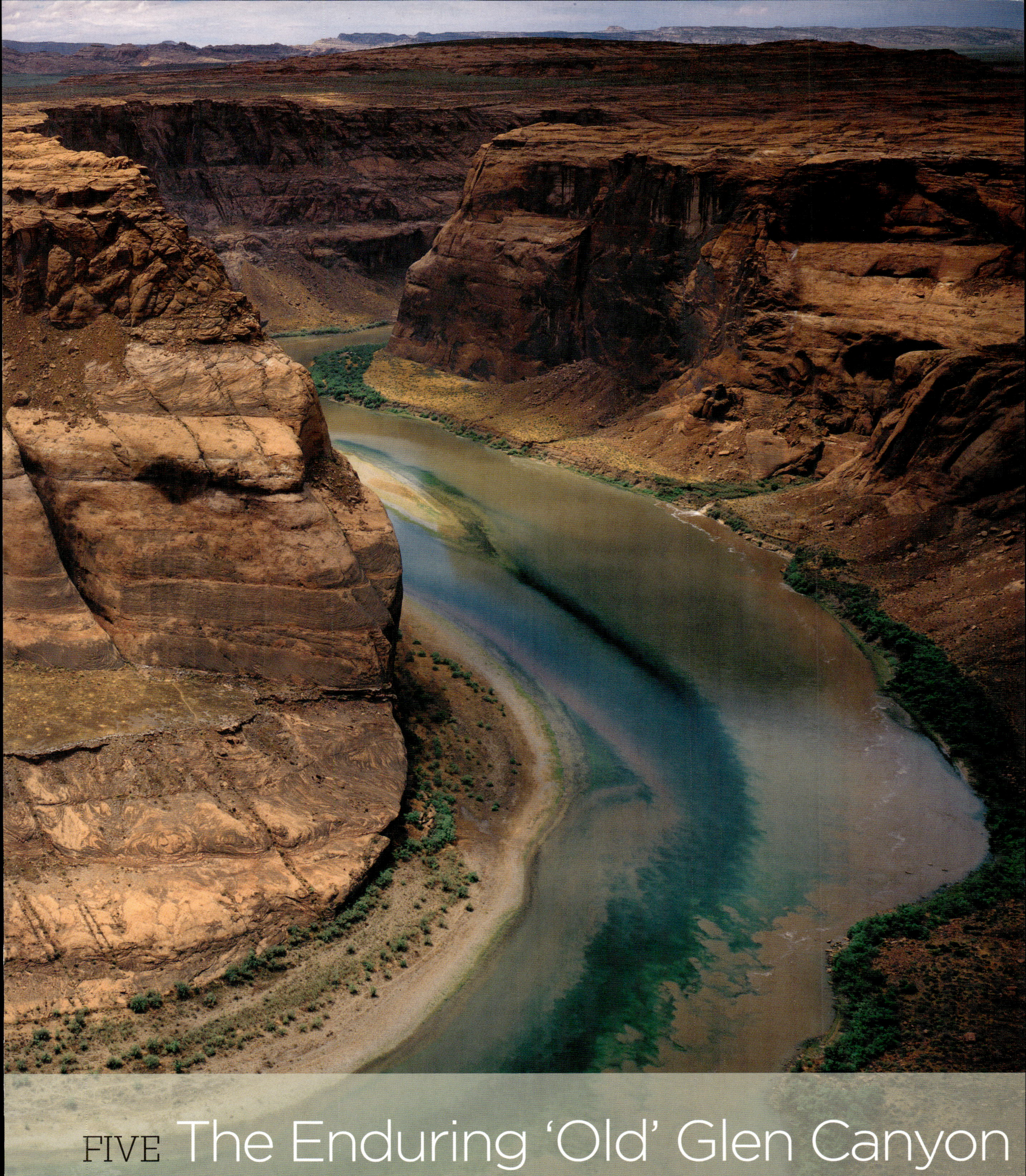

# FIVE The Enduring 'Old' Glen Canyon

# FIVE The Enduring 'Old' Glen Canyon

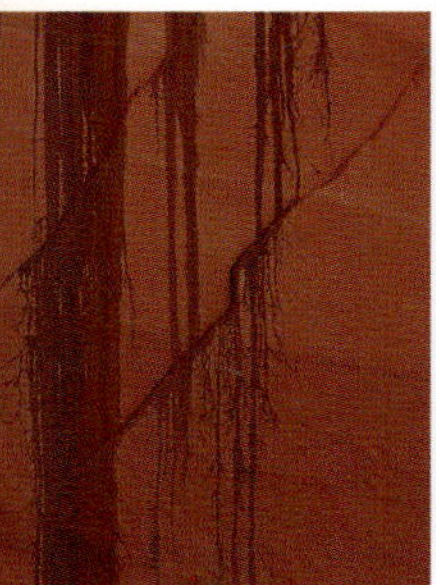

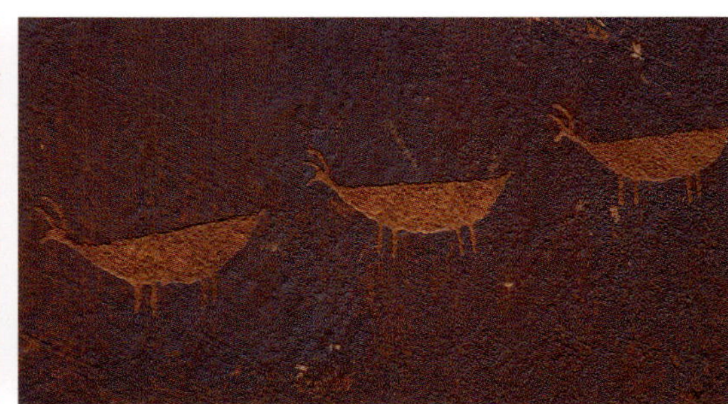

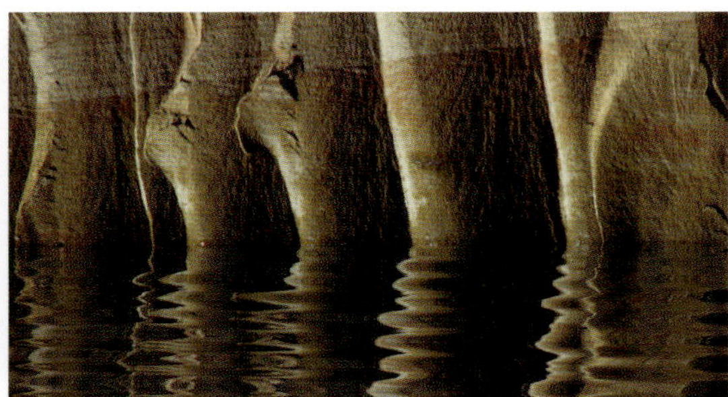

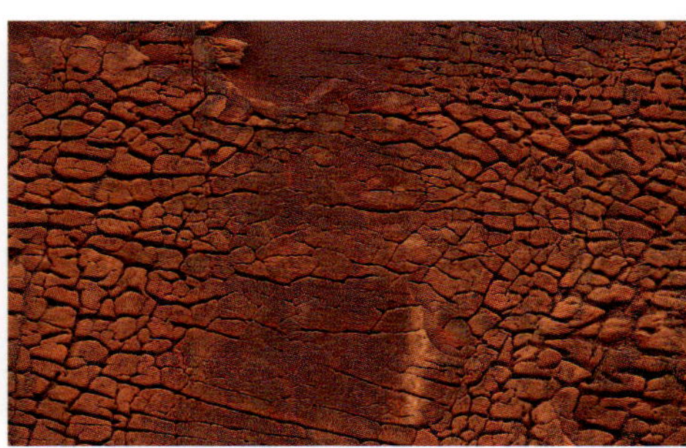

A small launch ramp was once located at the base of Glen Canyon Dam. For several years, about once each year, my fellow river-runner friends and I launched three wooden dories from the old ramp.

Once on the water, we floated quietly down Glen Canyon, wet oars flashing in the sun, oarlocks squeaking with every tug. Great blue herons glided by, spring waters trickled from cracks in the cliffs, beavers slapped their tails at the sight of us. We visited petroglyph panels, scrambled up side canyons, photographed patterns of conchoidal fracture, examined at close range the blooms of claretcup hedgehog cacti, and bathed in the essence of "old" Glen Canyon. For three leisurely days, we floated along on the fifteen miles of Colorado River from the base of the dam to Lee's Ferry, our slow pace providing the time needed to savor this one surviving shard of untrammeled Glen Canyon.

These were wonderful trips. Sadly, the launch ramp was destroyed by the extreme flows of the Colorado River in the early summer of 1983, and our peaceful dory retreats came to an end.

But I still boat old Glen Canyon. In 1995 I purchased a used inflatable raft and motor specifically to continue my photography in this ancient Glen Canyon corridor. Now I launch at Lee's Ferry and motor upstream, find a campsite, spend the night, and float and motor back downstream the following day, taking pictures whenever appropriate. The last time I did this, I had company along and the monsoon rains drenched us as we motored away from our launch point. Upstream, multiple silver waterfalls plunged from the rims. And the next morning, gossamer fog lay upon the river.

Left to right: **Desert varnish and mud stains** adorn a wall of Entrada Sandstone.
**Ancestral Puebloan petroglyphs** were found along the Colorado River in "old" Glen Canyon.
**An undulating rock wall** is reflected at the edge of Padre Bay.
**A sandstone cliff** in Escalante Canyon displays weathering.

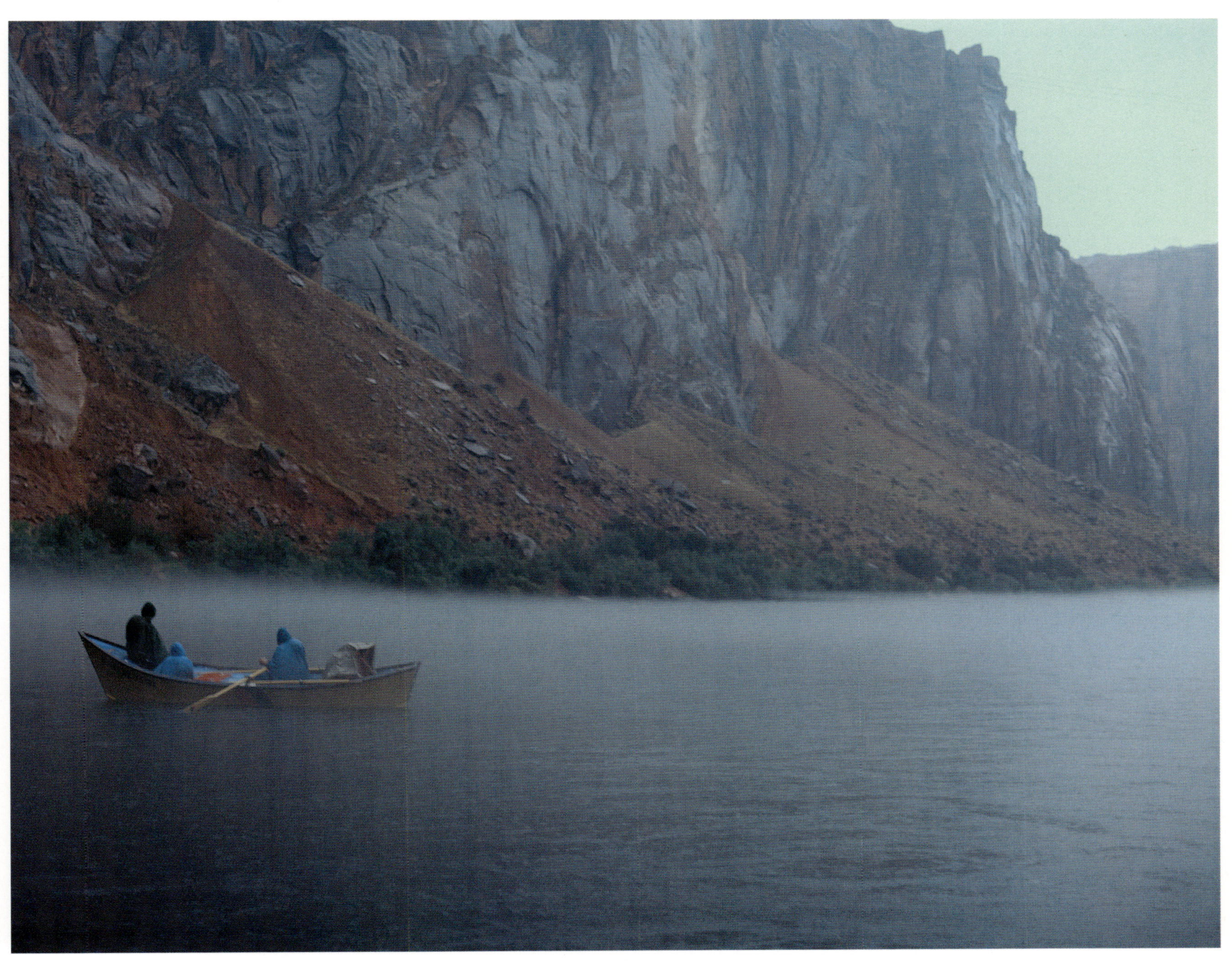

**Passengers of a dory** wear rain gear during a summer rain as they float the Colorado River downstream from Glen Canyon Dam. Because the Colorado River's flow is drawn from deep within Lake Powell, its waters run surprisingly cold year-round, about 47 degrees F. In the summer when the air is often both warm and moist, a foggy mist materializes to envelop river boats and shoreline vegetation.

## A Jewel of a Canyon

The old Glen Canyon is still there, truncated and sandwiched between the playground of luxury houseboats upstream and the whitewater rafts and dories of Grand Canyon downstream. Today its waters run clear and the shorelines are crowded with tamarisk trees. But this stretch of river remains a haven, a tranquil ribbon of refreshment meandering through the desert. Copper-colored sandstone cliffs loom a thousand feet or higher above, and morning sunlight bounces off the east-facing cliffs, painting the opposite shorelines in shades of orange and gold.

Even in summer, when air temperatures sometimes top 100 degrees, the river runs cold — cold enough for swimmers to become hypothermic in minutes, and clear enough for its cobbled bed and sandy floor to be visible far below the surface. Crystalline water and cold temperatures were not part of Glen Canyon's many charms before the dam.

It's easy to understand why the hearts of those who floated the full sweep of Glen Canyon were shattered by the intrusion of Glen Canyon Dam. There's nothing comparable to the pleasure of gliding along on the powerful, ceaseless currents of an age-old river. Even today, on the float downstream, quitting the river at the Lee's Ferry dock seems cruel. One wants to continue into yet more canyons, more adventures, more wonders.

Major John Wesley Powell was the first to systematically explore the Green and Colorado rivers. He and his men drifted in three boats through this stretch of Glen Canyon on August 4, 1869. A day earlier, they had identified the location of the Crossing of the Fathers (an ancient river crossing that today lies beneath the waters of Padre Bay), and the next day they would enter Grand Canyon's gateway just downstream from what would soon become Lee's Ferry.

Powell was an explorer and scientist, and later a government bureaucrat. And he was astonishingly skilled with his pen. His book, *The Exploration of the Colorado River and its Canyons,* is regarded as a Colorado River bible. His descriptions of the canyons remain unsurpassed:

> *On the walls, and back many miles into the country, numbers of monument-shaped buttes are observed. So we have a curious ensemble of wonderful features — carved walls, royal arches, glens, alcove gulches, mounds and monuments. From which of these features shall we select a name? We decide to call it Glen Canyon.*

It would be impossible to find a more fitting name for this peaceful, sensually carved, friendly, and beautiful canyon. Powell continued:

> *Past these towering monuments, past these mounded billows of orange sandstone, past these oak-set glens, past these fern-decked alcoves, past these mural curves, we glide hour after hour, stopping now and then, as our attention is arrested by some new wonder.*

This is the charm of today's Glen Canyon, too — both on the river downstream of the dam and upstream, beyond the lake's reach. One is always looking for some feature of known interest, only to be "arrested by some new wonder."

Above: **Grasses, a sacred datura, and a sandstone cliff** glow in diffuse light reflected from old Glen Canyon's towering cliffs. Because Glen Canyon Dam limits the size of floods allowed to rip through the lower end of Glen Canyon and Grand Canyon, much of the river corridor's vegetation and wildlife has changed.

Right: **Six miles upstream from Lee's Ferry,** near one proposed location for Glen Canyon Dam, morning sun crowns the towering walls of Glen Canyon. Downstream the Colorado River bends left, then begins to carve a huge loop back to the right, ending its meander at Lee's Ferry less than a mile from this location immediately behind the cliff on right side.

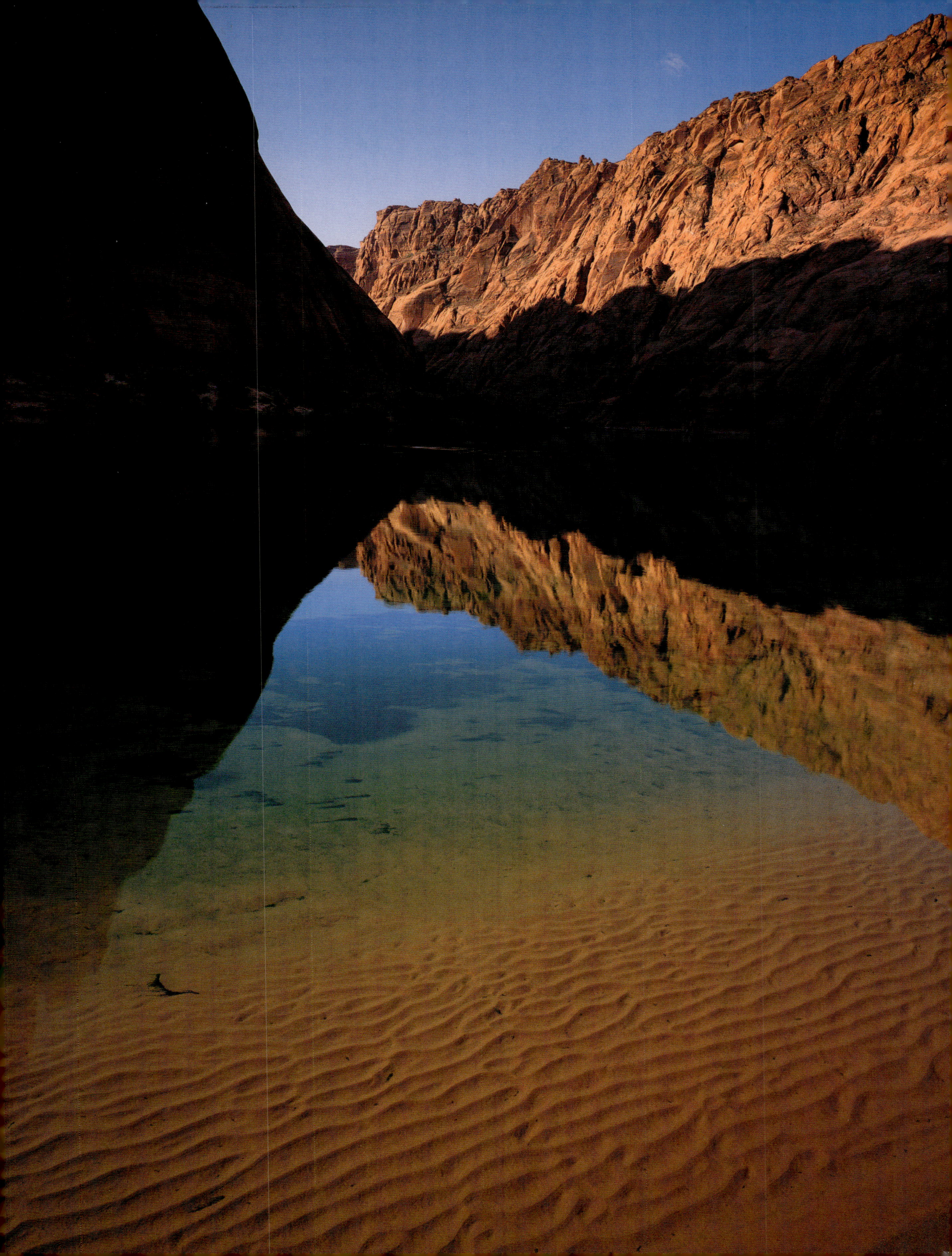

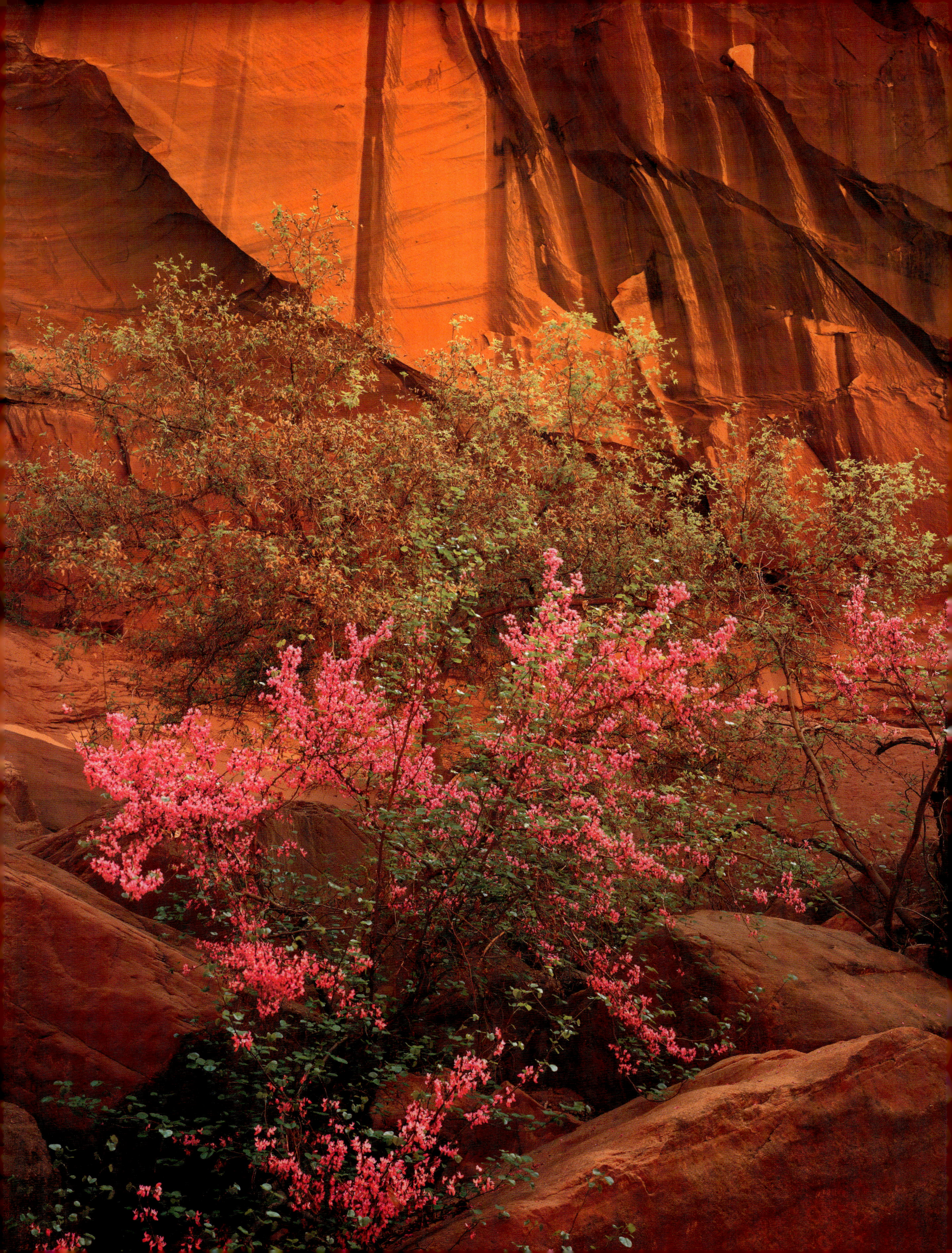

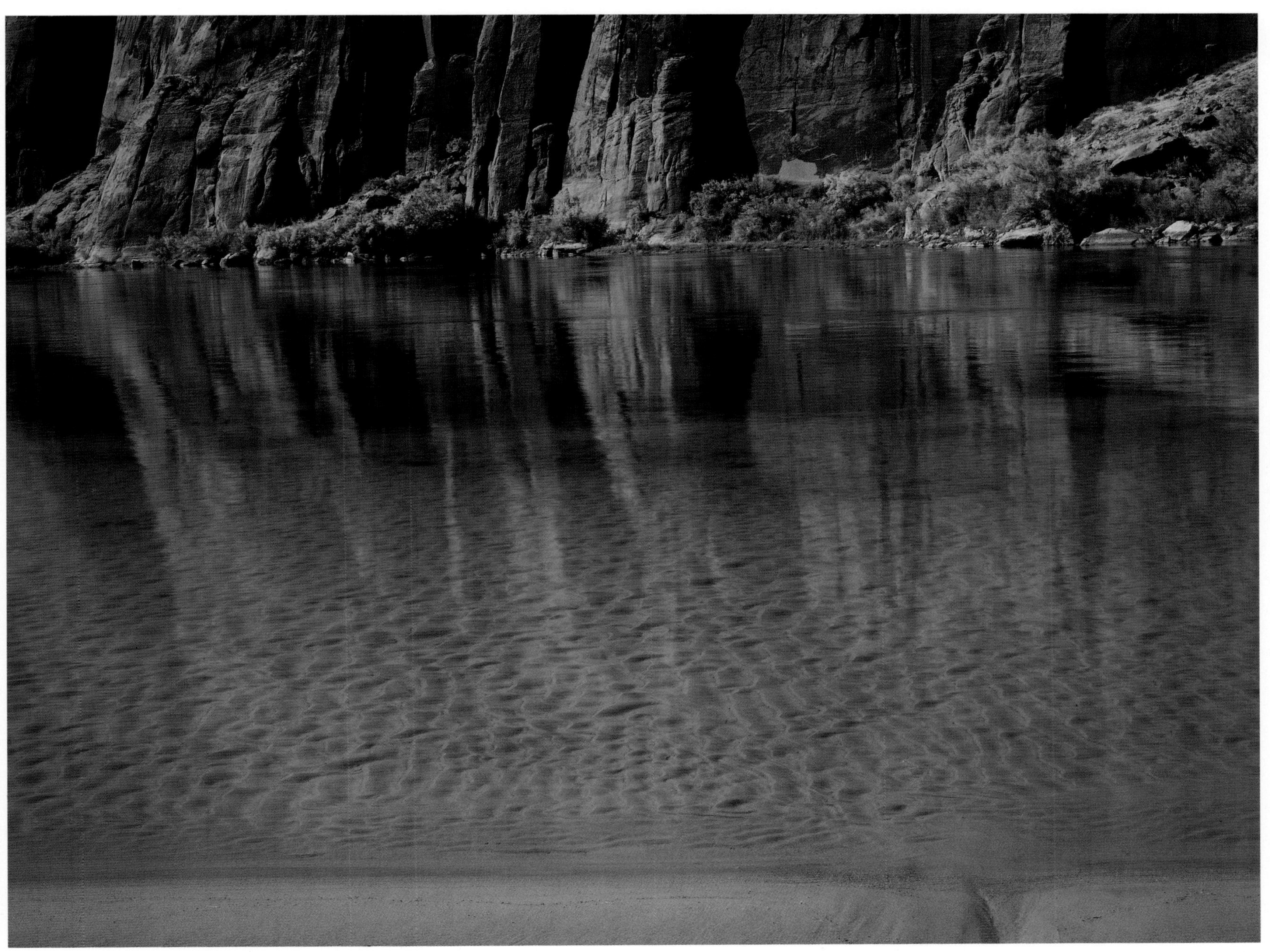

Left: **Approaching Glen Canyon's end,** side canyons become infrequent. But there are a couple of beauties just upstream of Lee's Ferry. One is Waterholes Canyon. Here, bright pink blooms of redbud trees compete with the glowing orange color of patina-draped cliffs.

Above: **Reflections dominate on the placid Colorado River** in Glen Canyon. Before Lake Powell's creation, the Colorado River flowed 150 miles, the full length of Glen Canyon, on an extremely gentle gradient.

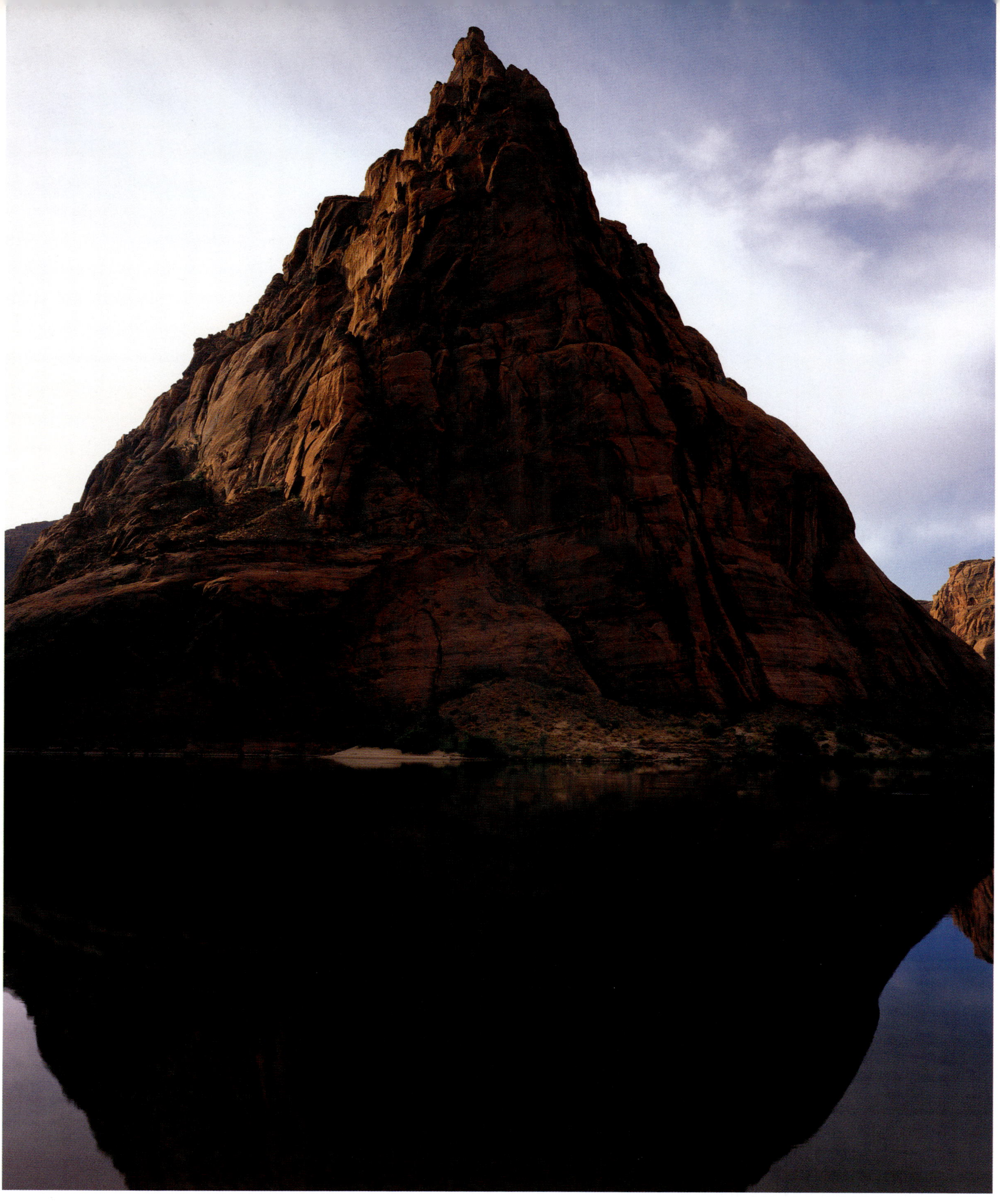

Above: **Near this location in old Glen Canyon,** about nine miles downstream from the dam, dinosaur footprints were found on a ledge of limestone jutting out from the canyon wall.

Right, above: **Curving lines of a conchoidal fracture** adorn the base of a sandstone cliff near river mile seven in old Glen Canyon.

Right, below: **Late-afternoon light in mid-April** backlights prince's plume near river mile eight in old Glen Canyon.

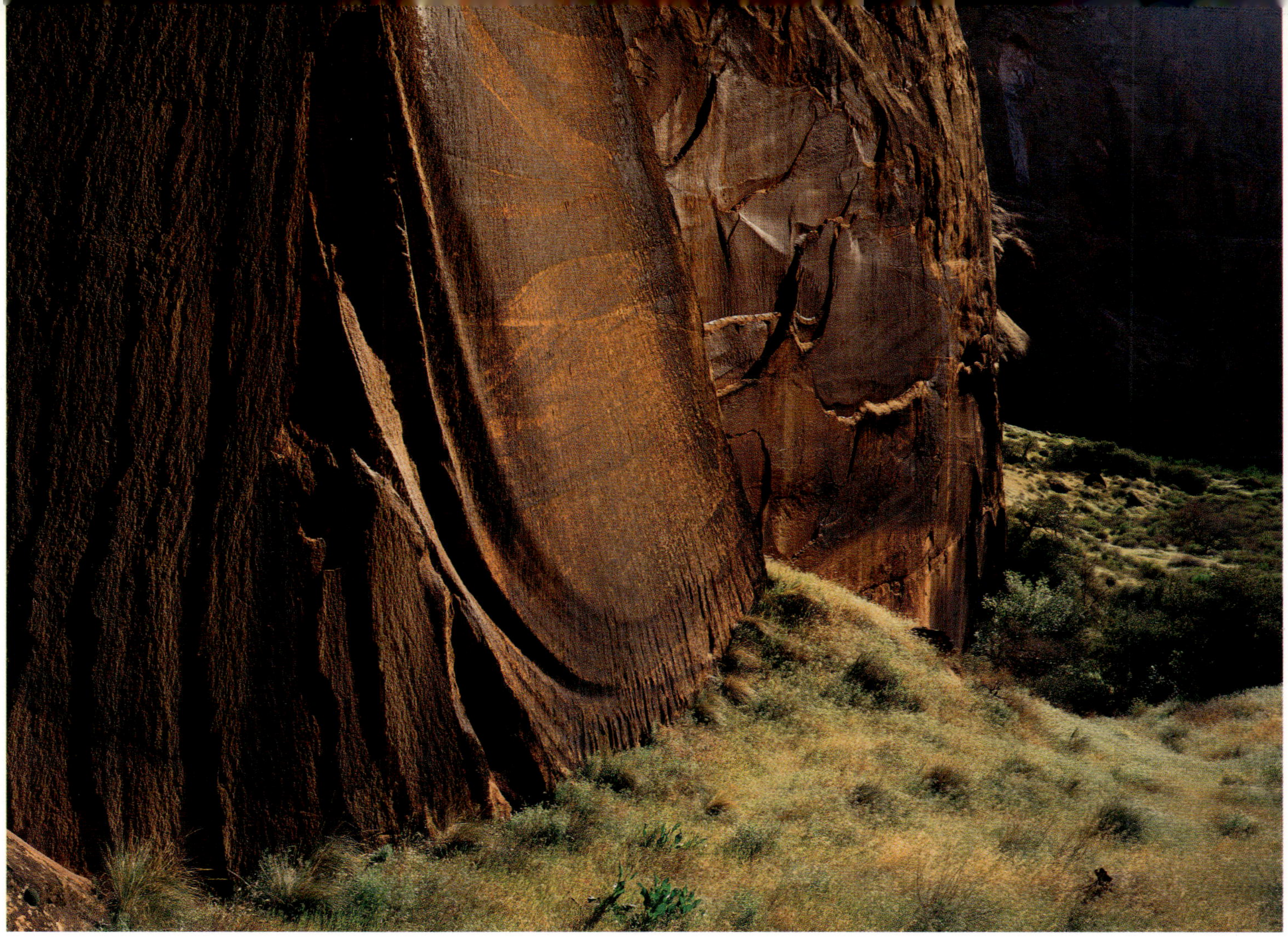

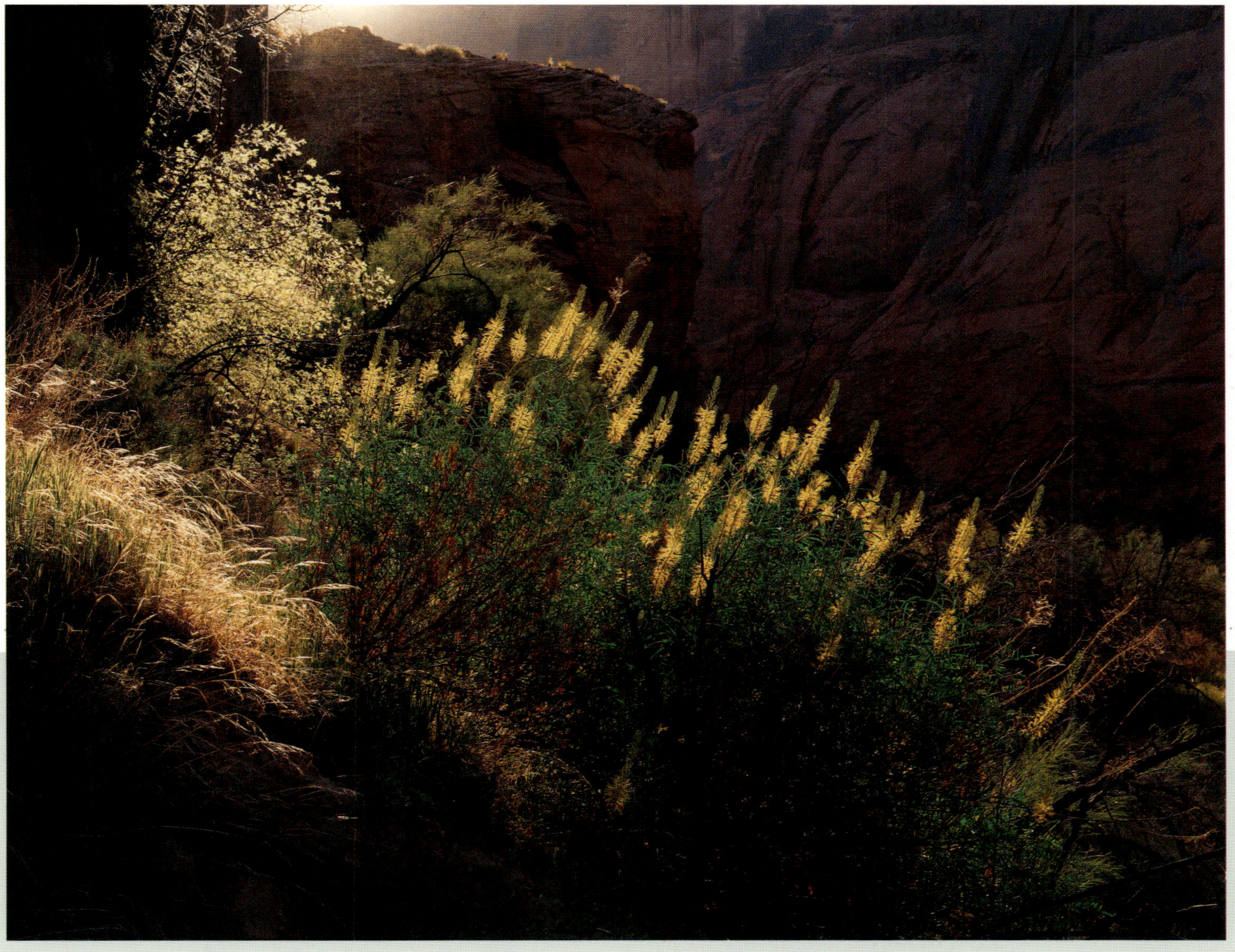

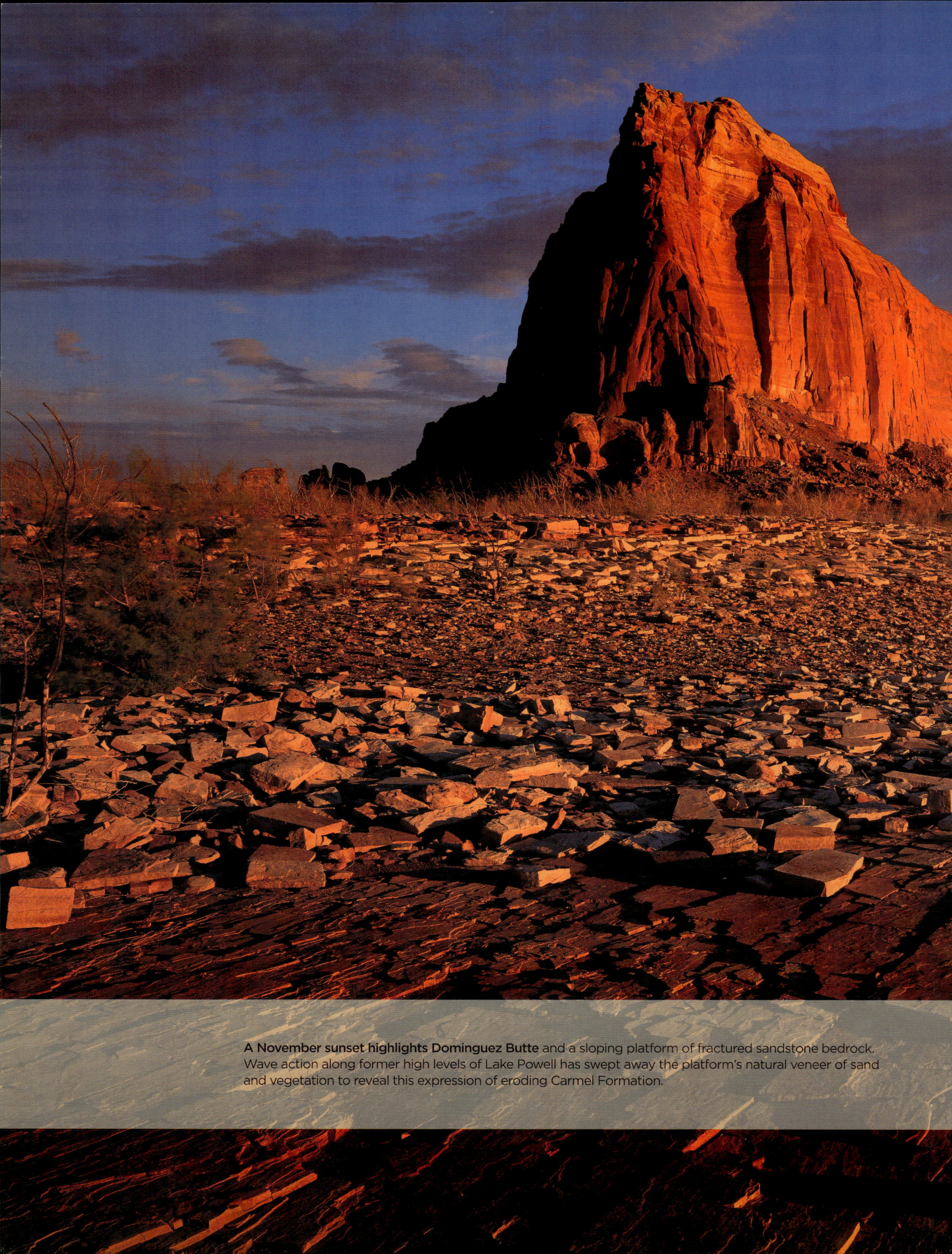

**A November sunset highlights Dominguez Butte** and a sloping platform of fractured sandstone bedrock. Wave action along former high levels of Lake Powell has swept away the platform's natural veneer of sand and vegetation to reveal this expression of eroding Carmel Formation.

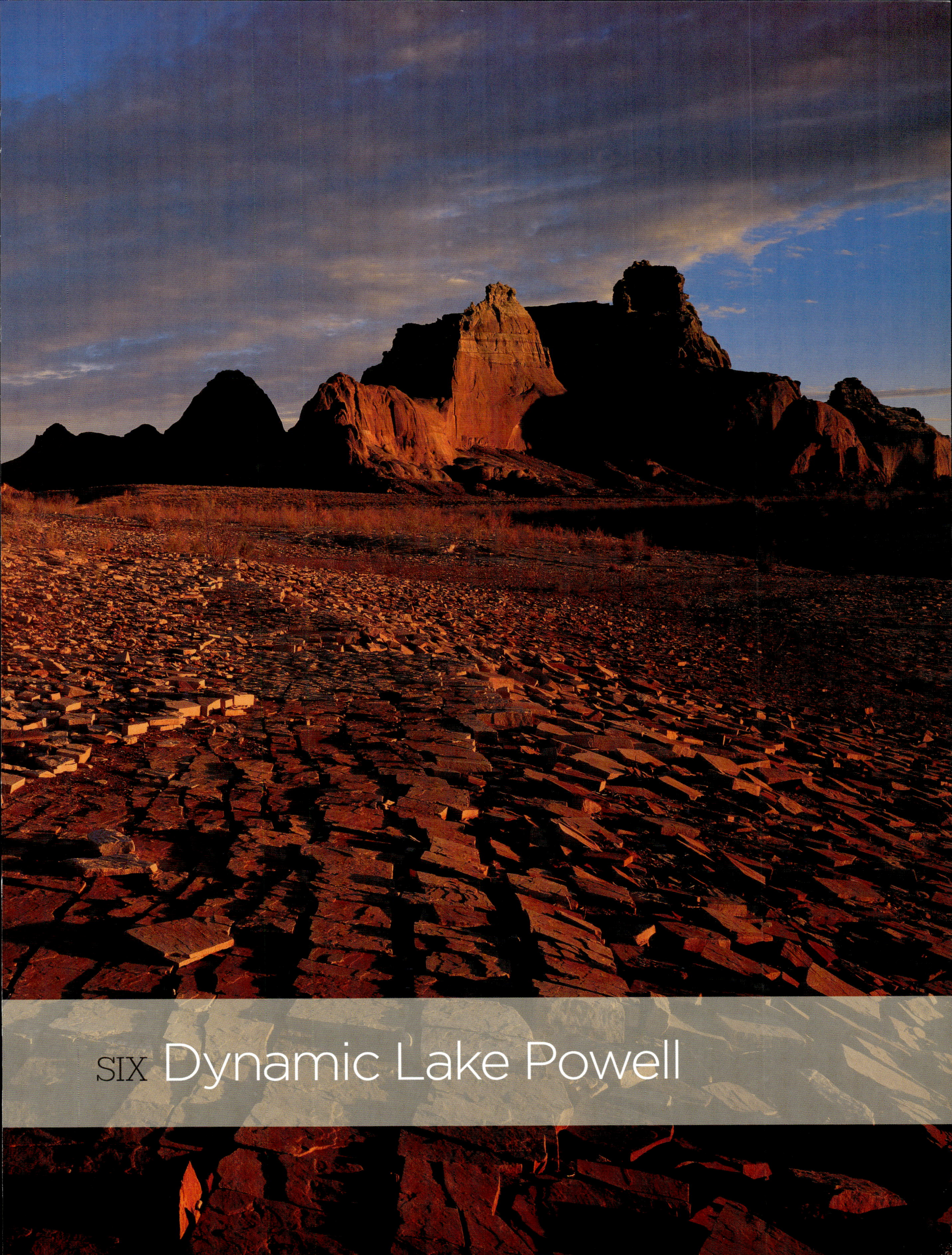

# SIX Dynamic Lake Powell

# SIX Dynamic Lake Powell

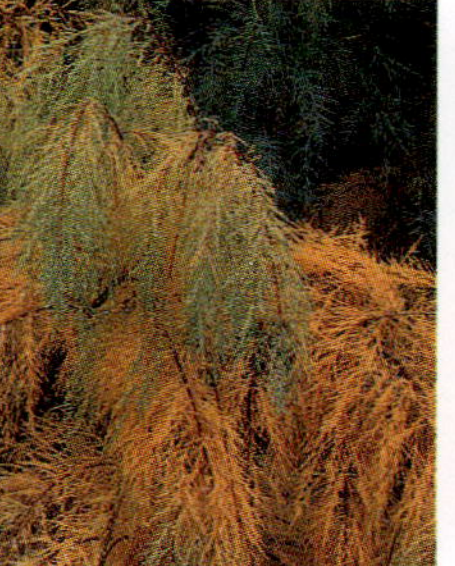
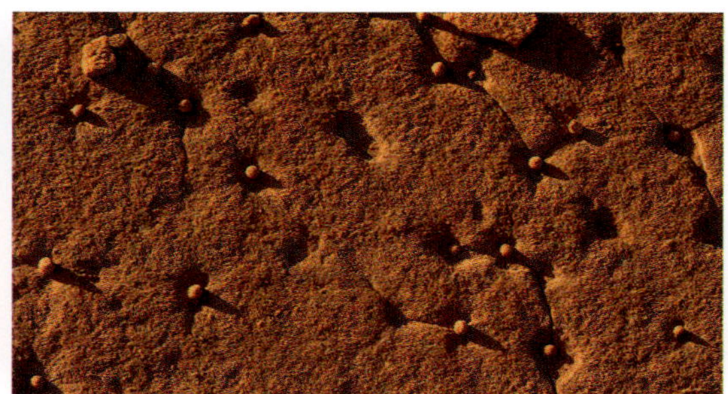
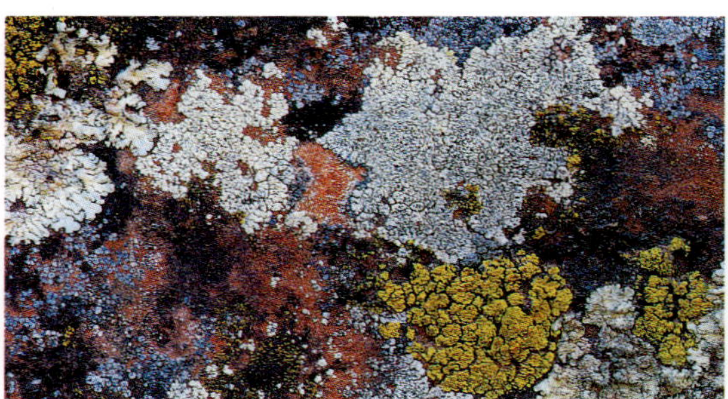
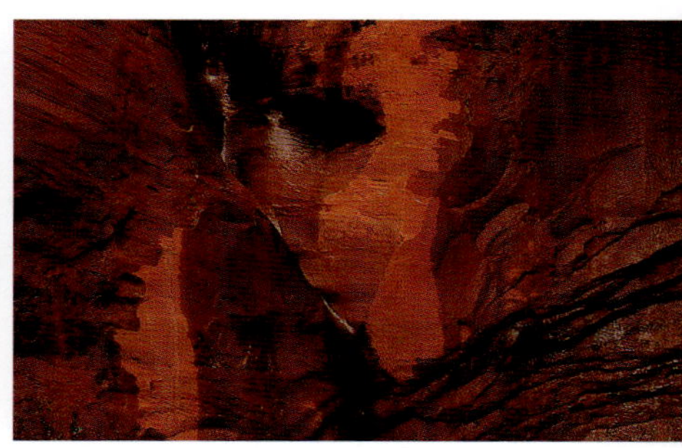

While hiking upstream in Cascade Canyon, a tributary of Lake Powell, a fellow hiker mentioned that the seven-foot-high boulder obstacle we had just surmounted with some difficulty was buried in sand and gravel to within a foot of its rounded top only a year or two before. Falling lake levels had recently dewatered this section of canyon, allowing flash floods to once again begin moving sand and smaller rocks downstream. But the big boulder had remained wedged between the walls, while the smaller rubble downstream from it had been swept away.

A week later, following several days of rare October downpours, we again visited Cascade Canyon, hiking upstream from lake's end to the same troublesome boulder. Now, the scene had been transformed. The boulder was still there but the floods had carried away the sand, gravel, and cobbles that had been jammed behind and below it. The boulder became a hanging chockstone. So, instead of climbing over it, we easily walked under it.

Left to right: **Tamarisks** wear fall color near Ferry Swale on the Colorado River.
**Sandstone** is shown in detail in Labyrinth Canyon.
**Lichens** in Escalante Canyon paint a sandstone cliff in pastel colors.
**Rock walls** in Lehi Canyon.

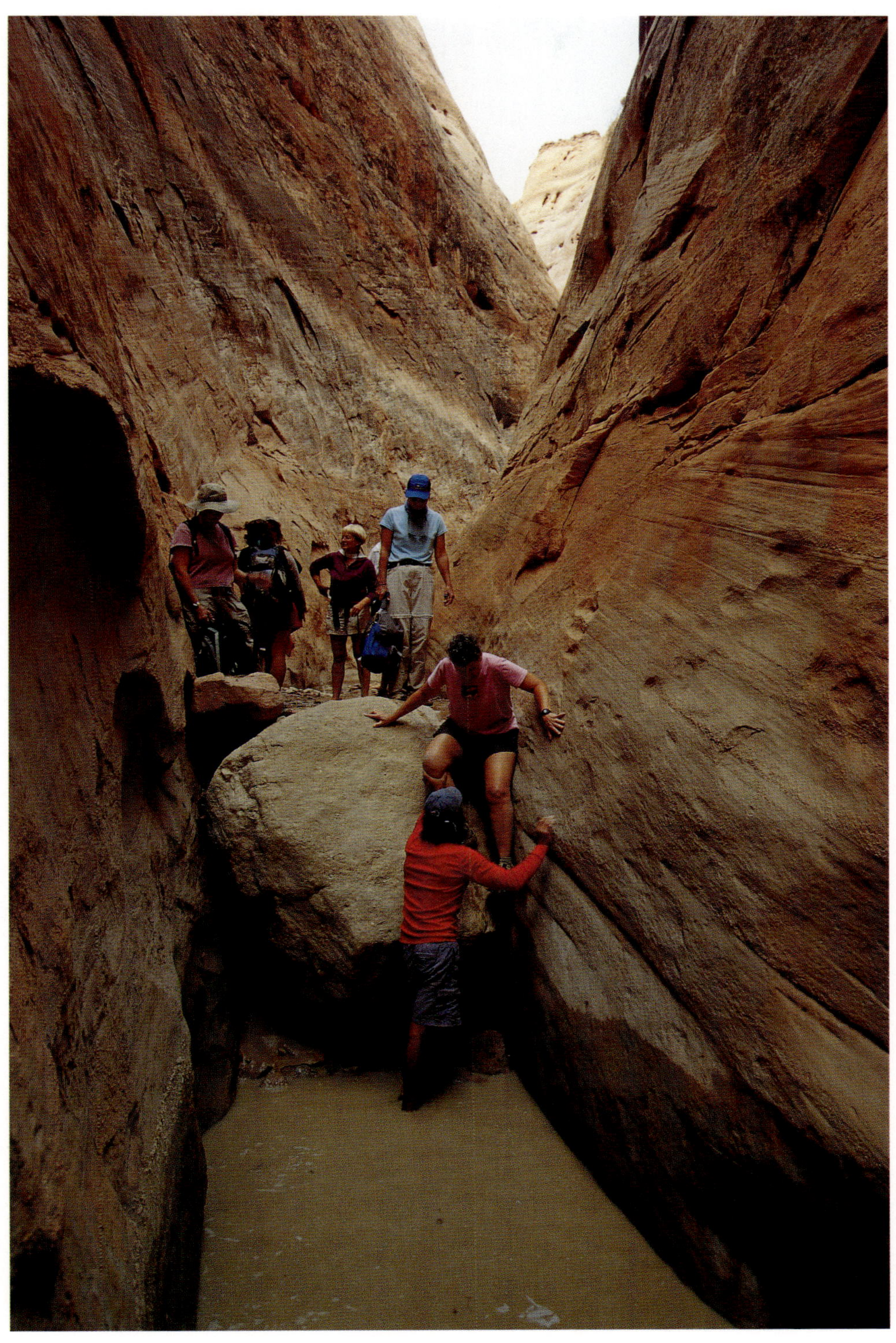

**Day-hikers in Cascade Canyon** negotiate a chockstone obstacle. One of the joys of Lake Powell is its astonishing array of side canyon environments. Some are cool and shady slot canyons; others are broad and exposed to the sun. Some host perennial streams, while others rarely see a dribble of flowing water. Some offer easy walking, and others are clogged with vegetation.

## Changing Shorelines, Transformed Canyons

The creation of Lake Powell unbalanced an ancient, natural equilibrium that existed in Glen Canyon.

Before the lake, sand and cobbles, weathered from the cliffs and slopes of side canyons, were carried to the Colorado River by gravity, flash floods, and debris flows. Small rapids sometimes formed at the mouths of side canyons where the Colorado River choked on recently delivered rubble. The rubble remained there until the Colorado River itself swelled with spring snowmelt waters. Then, much of the refuse tumbled away to be dissolved and pulverized by the river's powerful flow.

After Lake Powell inundated Glen Canyon, the rules changed. The energetic Colorado River has been swamped by the waters of a deep and tranquil lake. Flash floods, occasionally roaring down the side canyons as before, still transport sand and rock, but now they dump it into the lake's still waters. There's no Colorado River to cart it away.

Instead, at lake's edge within the side canyons, deltas of sand and silt grow in size, pushing down-canyon. When the lake elevation falls, side canyon streams once again begin to urge the sand and stone toward the lake's retreating shore. There's a kind of quiet war in progress between the waters of the formidable lake and the waters of steadfast streams.

Lake Powell's surface elevation fluctuations are substantial. April through July of the average year will usually see the lake's surface rise twenty to thirty feet. Then, in most years, the lake surrenders about the same amount of elevation during the rest of the year. Overly wet or dry years magnify the fluctuations. Such dramatic level changes are expected at Lake Powell. The lake retains high flows so that excess water can be released and utilized later during dry months or drought years.

But for recreational users of Lake Powell, lake level changes can be disturbing, even disorienting. Islands come and go. Favorite campsites are drowned or left high and dry. Where once there was a cliff, now there's an alcove; where once there was a bay, now there's a twisting inlet; where once there was a rugged talus of sharp boulders, now there's a superb beach.

At full volume, Lake Powell's convoluted shoreline measures 1,900 miles. When the lake loses thirty, forty, fifty feet in elevation, an entirely new shoreline materializes, unveiling still more of the lost Glen Canyon topography (and a windfall of new terrain for photographers). When the lake's level rises it invents fresh interplays between stone and water, making still more new images possible.

## Long-Term Outlook

On a longer time scale, Lake Powell is wildly dynamic. Like all lakes, both artificial and natural, Lake Powell will gradually fill with sand, silt, and cobbles. Lake Powell's two major tributary rivers, the Colorado and the San Juan, along with its smaller side canyon streams, are the responsible parties. Scientists believe that the lake will completely fill with silt in 500 to 700 years.

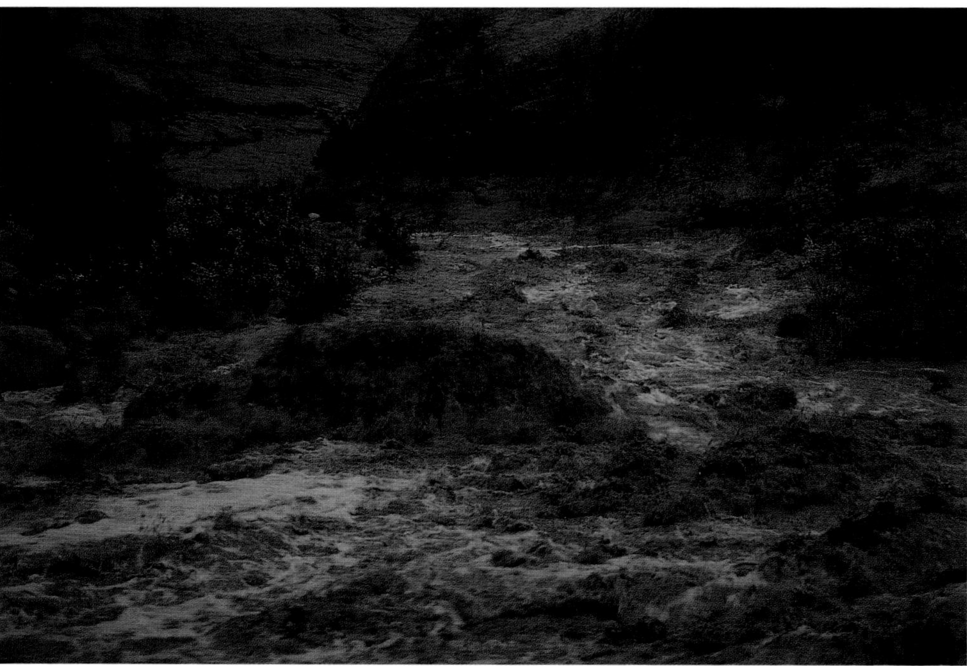

**Flash-flood waters race down Cliff Canyon** to hurdle a boulder and join a separate flood rumbling down Forbidding Canyon. The photo was made from my campsite during a backpack trip. Close to 1,000 cubic feet of muddy water roared by each second — roughly 5 to 10 percent of a typical Colorado River flow.

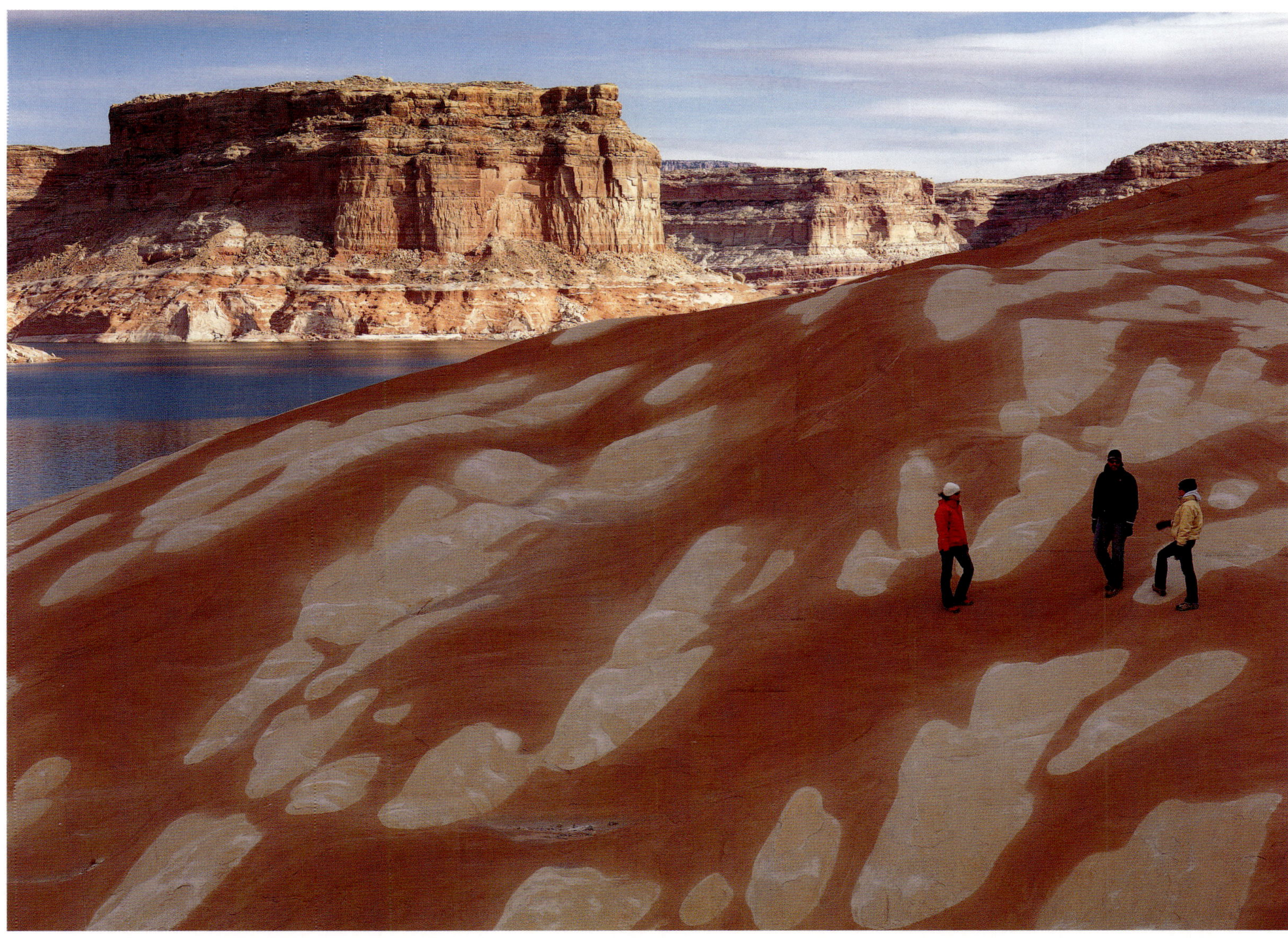

To halt or reverse the slow demise of Lake Powell would be a worthy goal. Dredging is a possible solution, but not a good one. We can't dredge fast enough — on average, the equivalent of 10,000 15-cubic-foot dump-truck loads of silt pour into Lake Powell every day.

The siltation of Lake Powell is worrisome, and the dam's powerful influence on the Colorado River downstream is regrettable. On the other hand, our world is loaded down with far bigger environmental problems that loom ever larger, including overpopulation, overfishing of oceans, pollution, climate change, and resource depletions of many kinds. Lake Powell's troubles are small in comparison.

Lake Powell will always evolve. Rockfalls and landslides will come, sometimes blocking side canyon arms of the lake. Upstream water-users will withdraw more and more water, to which they are entitled by law. That water would have otherwise bolstered the volume of Lake Powell. Times of drought and flood will come and go. We can count on the occurrence of the completely unanticipated. Lake Powell, for better and for worse, will continue to change and develop further complexities that will undoubtedly surprise and bedevil us.

**In late December, hikers explore** a unique outcrop of Entrada Sandstone in Last Chance Canyon. The unusual color patterns developed where circulating ground waters "reduced" the iron in the rock — coloring it white — while the rock still lay far below the surface. Recent uplift and erosion have brought the splotchy rock to the surface. When Lake Powell approaches full water level, this slickrock slope is completely inundated.

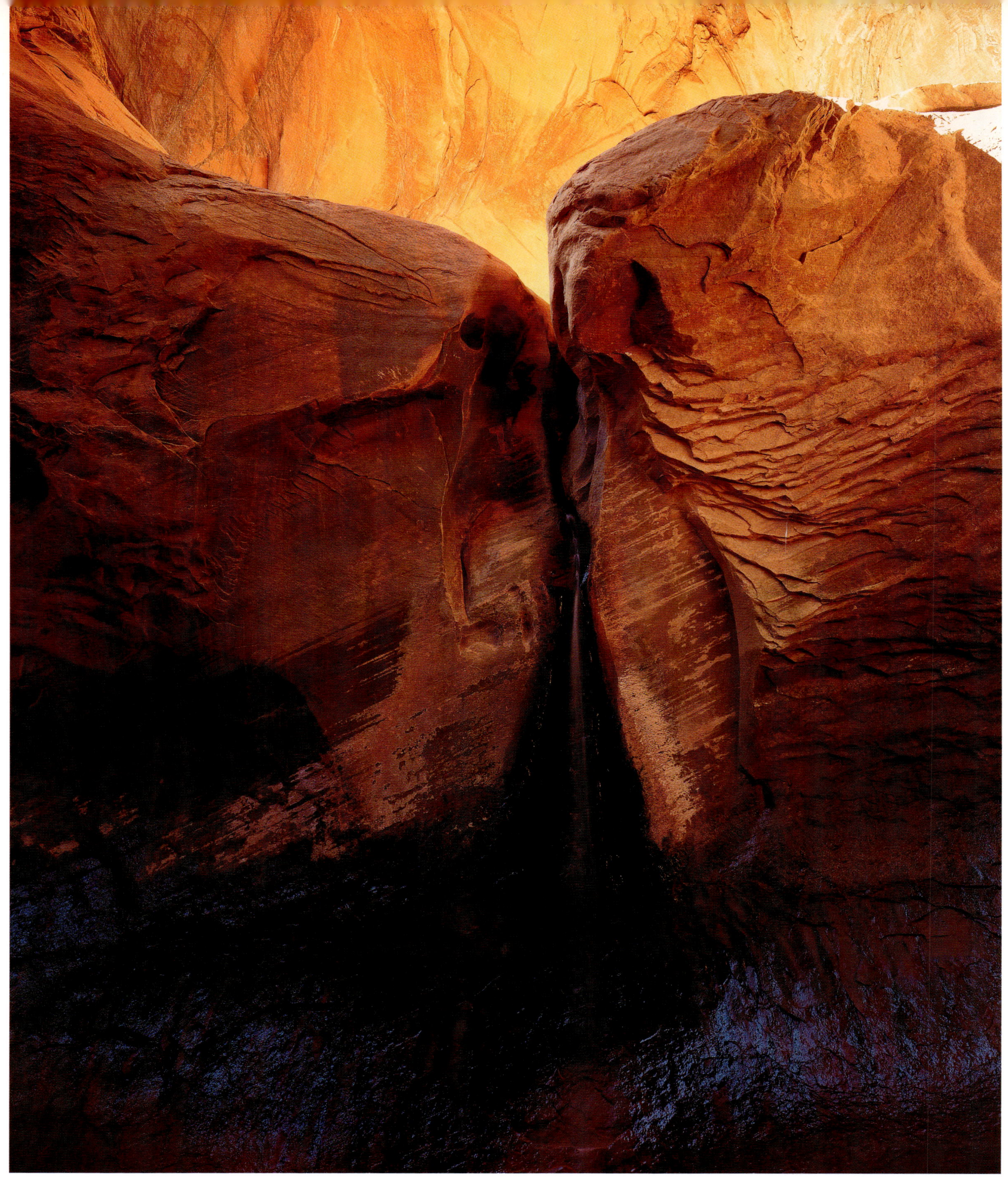

**If there was a heart of old Glen Canyon** before the creation of Lake Powell, it was probably Cathedral in the Desert, hidden in an Escalante Canyon tributary. Hikers turned a sharp corner to enter a soaring chamber carved from bedrock with only a narrow skylight twisting across in its ceiling, a little waterfall trickling into the room and an ambience of eternal, sublime beauty. Only when Lake Powell drops 150 feet below its full level does the Cathedral's floor come back to life.

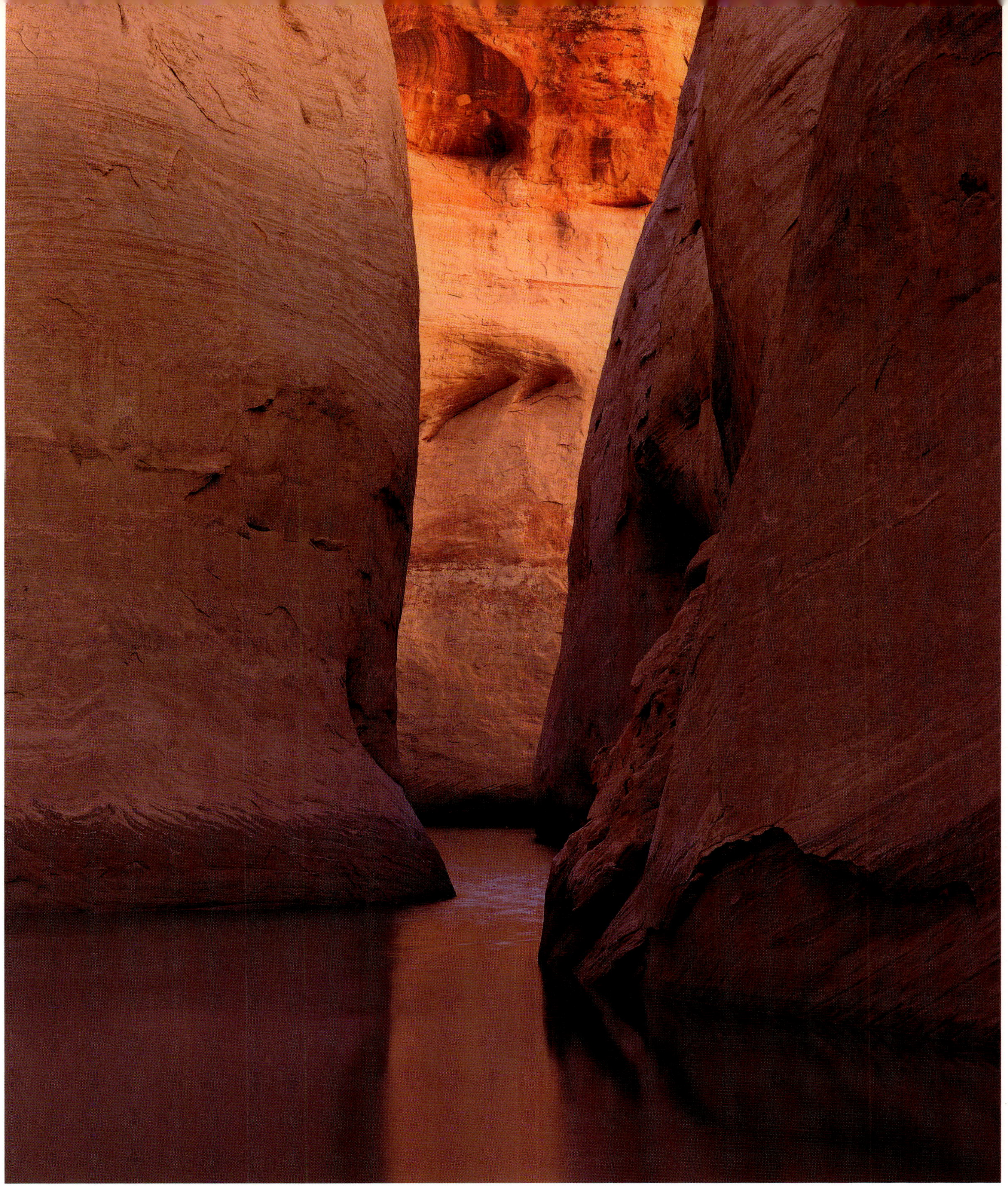

**Cascade Canyon is a favorite** of those who like to explore narrow canyons. The convoluted lower canyon is flooded by Lake Powell providing a formidable test of boating skills, and the dry upper reaches are a worthy test of arms and shoulders that must be used to surmount boulders and squirm up pouroffs.

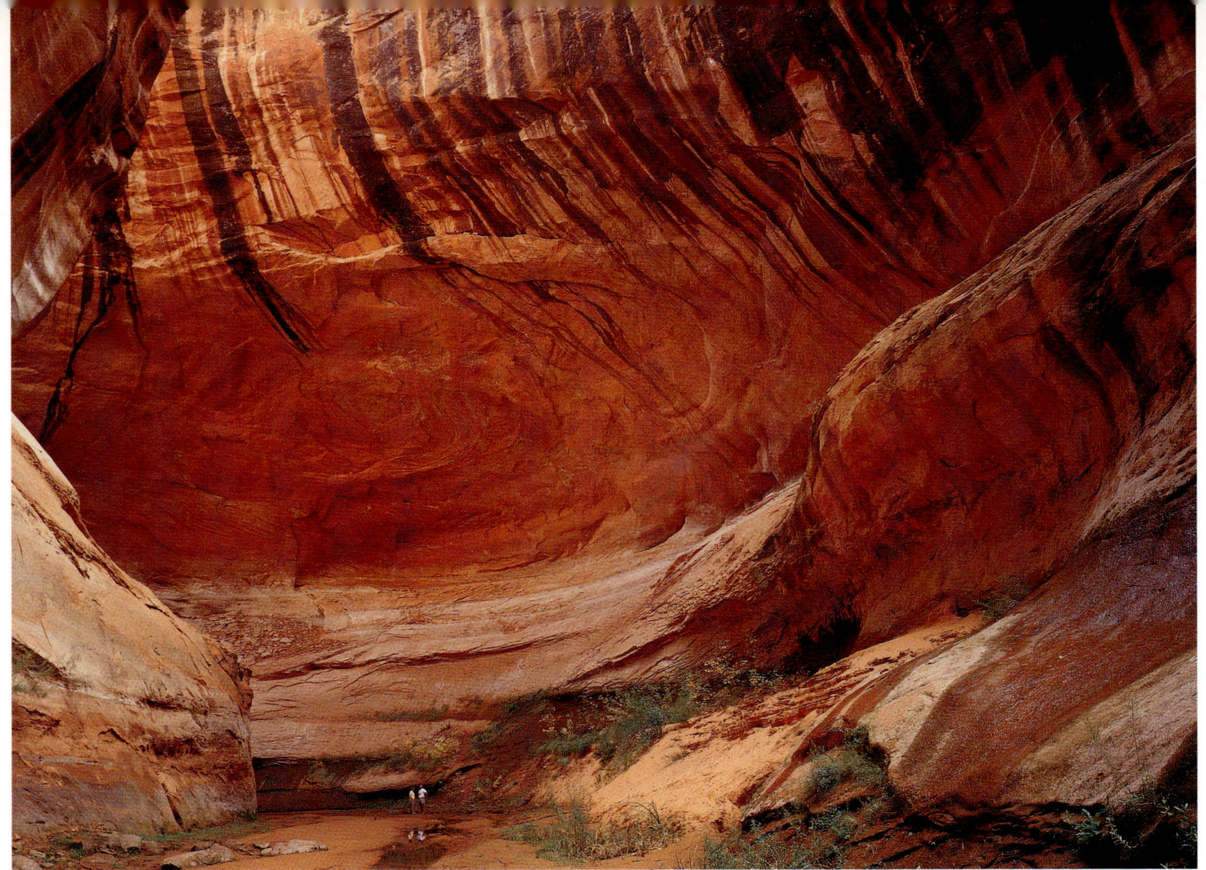

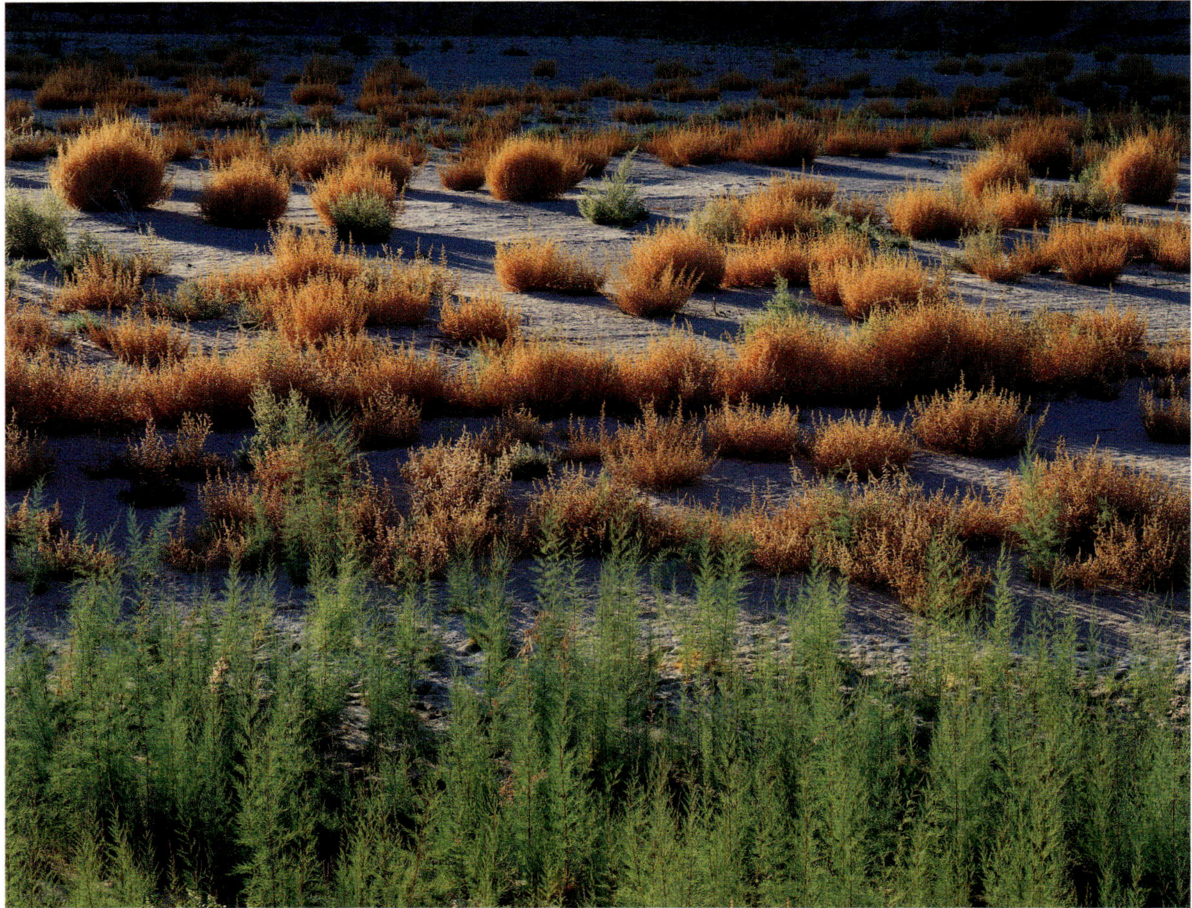

Top: **Hikers are dwarfed** by the massive overhanging walls of Clear Creek Canyon a short distance upstream from Cathedral in the Desert. As Lake Powell rises and falls, this chamber is alternately flooded then abandoned by the lake.

Above: **On average, almost 300 acres of land** are revealed with every one-foot drop in lake elevation. Of course, the "new" land is spread around the perimeter of the lake and much of it is steep slickrock. But where exposed land is sand and soil, plants invade, as here in Gunsight Canyon.

Right: **When Lake Powell dropped 80 feet** in the early 1990s, the San Juan River meandered across acres of thick silt beds that were deposited while the lake was high. The San Juan sliced a new channel downward into the soft silts until it ran into an old silt-covered canyon ridge of hard rock. As the lake continued to drop, a 25-foot waterfall developed at the edge of the resistant ridge. A few years later, a rising Lake Powell drowned the falls. When the lake dropped again after 1999, a new San Juan River waterfall appeared.

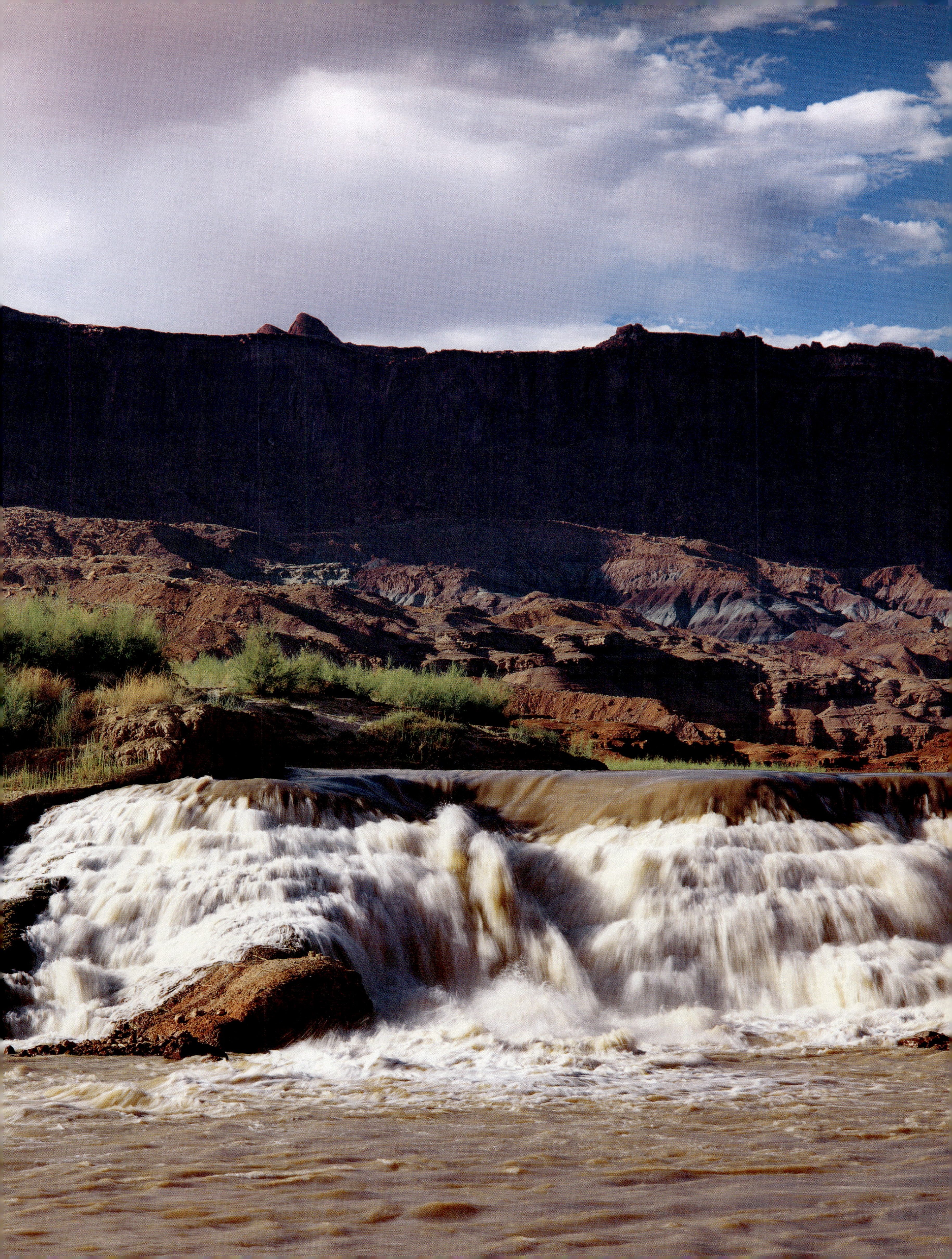

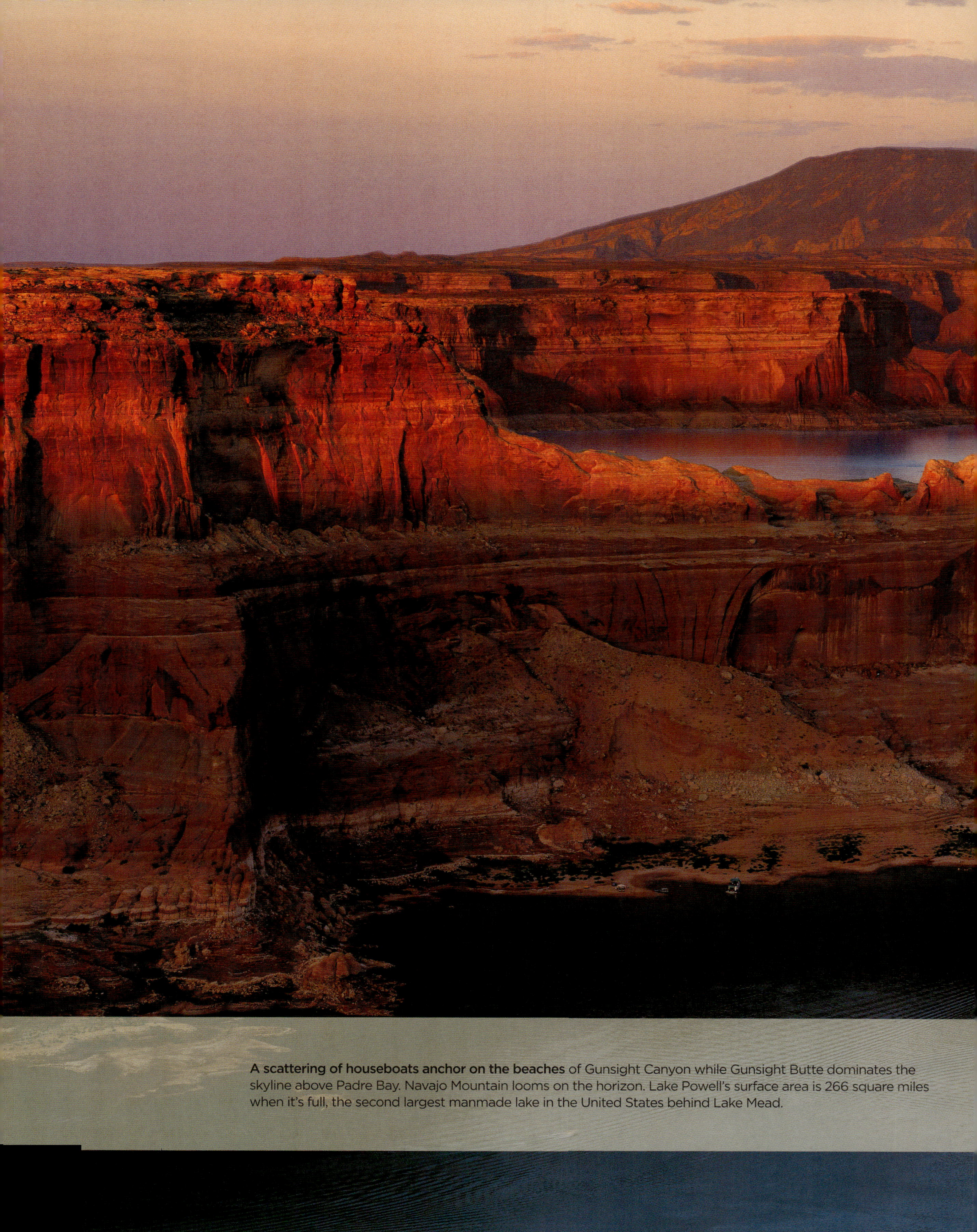

**A scattering of houseboats anchor on the beaches** of Gunsight Canyon while Gunsight Butte dominates the skyline above Padre Bay. Navajo Mountain looms on the horizon. Lake Powell's surface area is 266 square miles when it's full, the second largest manmade lake in the United States behind Lake Mead.

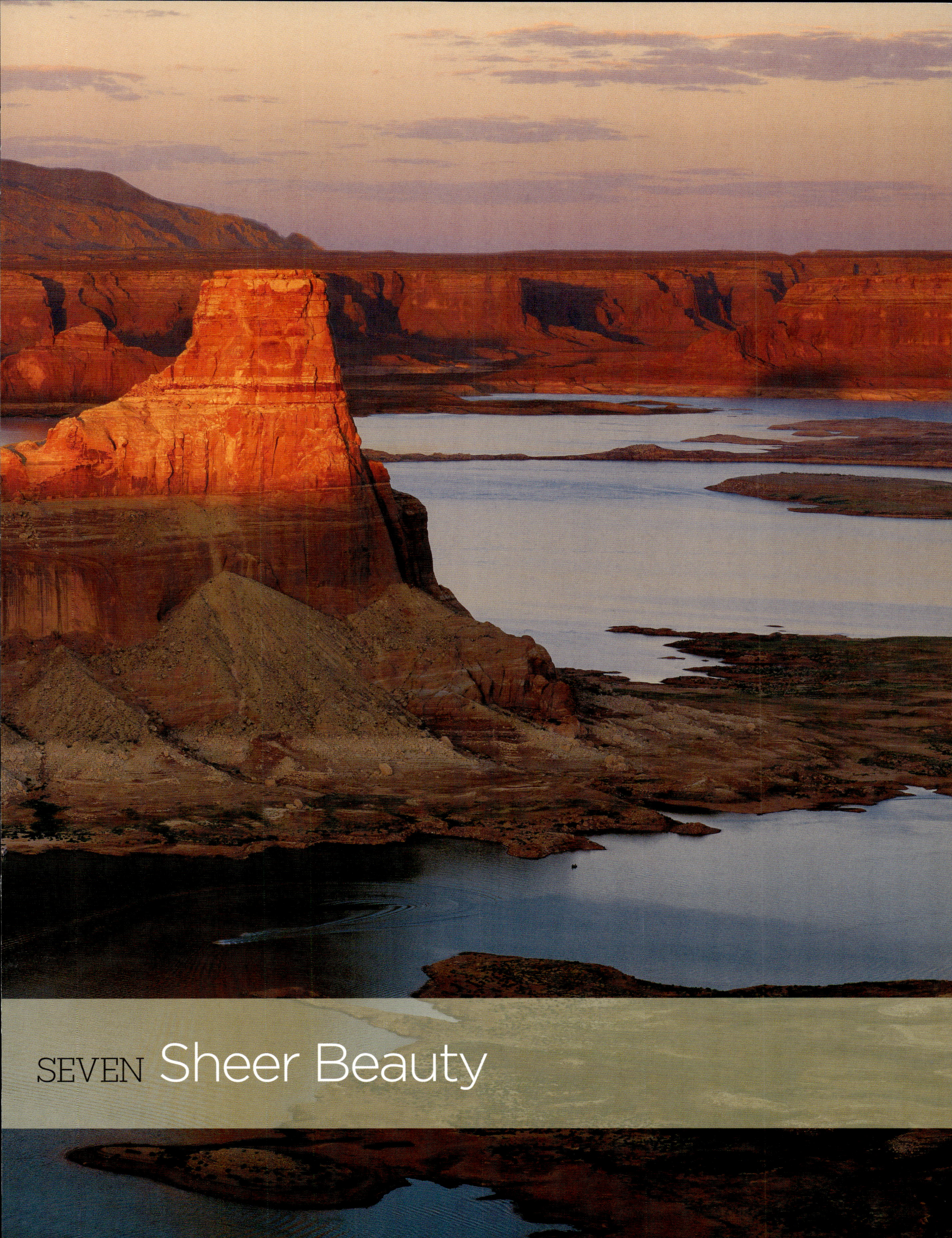

# SEVEN Sheer Beauty

# SEVEN Sheer Beauty

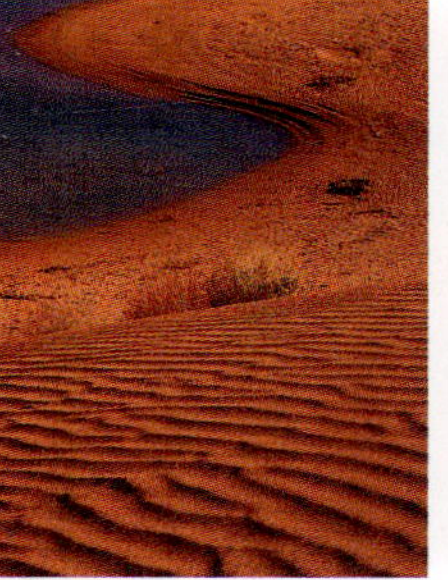
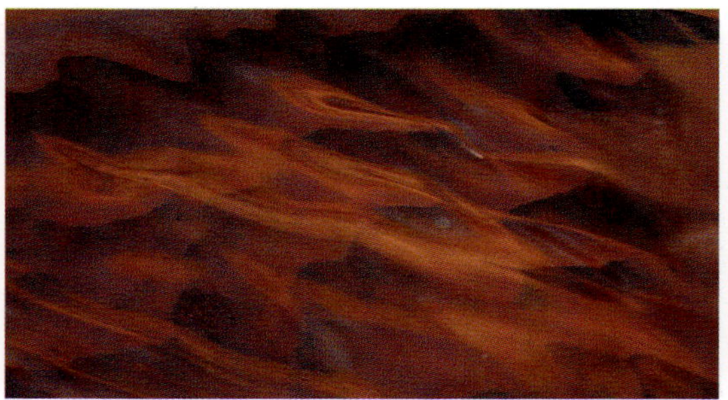
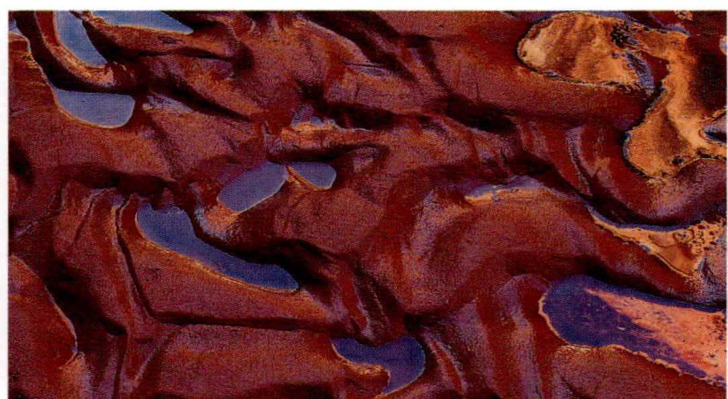
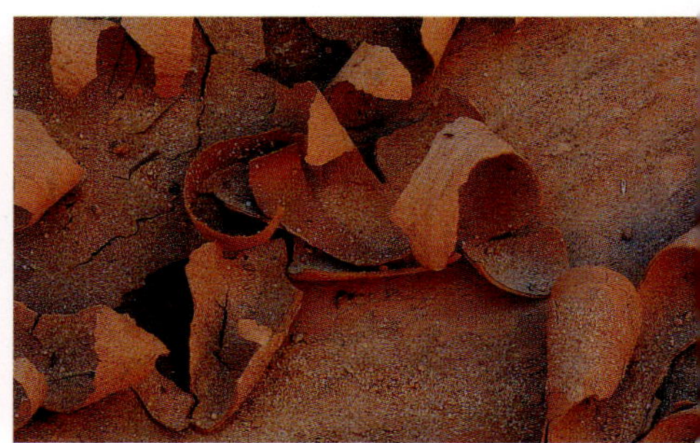

I'LL BET I'VE VISITED Alstrom Point, a Lake Powell overlook accessible by a rutted sand and dirt road, fifty times, maybe more. All those trips were made with the aim of catching the viewpoint's most photogenic moments, because the seasons, the clouds and their distribution, the hour, and the air transparency recombine in an infinity of combinations. The view from more than a thousand feet above the lake down into Gunsight Canyon and away toward Padre Bay and Navajo Mountain is sometimes phenomenally, extravagantly, absurdly fine. And that's just on an average day!

I've attended Alstrom Point sunsets when the location is more like a theater than an overlook. Off to the west, clouds block some beams of sunlight and refine others. Cosmic klieg lights and aerial spotlights illuminate only the most dramatic landscape props while subduing the backdrop here, highlighting important details there. The visual effects are sometimes so powerful that only with great difficulty can I concentrate on my camera, desiring rather to just sit and gawk.

One January morning, when it was too cold to sit and gawk, I witnessed and photographed what could be one of the most surreal sunrise scenes in the history of Planet Earth. It featured fog, white snow, blue snow, pink snow, mist, crepuscular rays, and mysterious shadows snaking across the landscape. The photograph appears on page 7, with Joe Alston's preface.

In the interest of full disclosure, let me admit that I've also attended Alstrom Point windstorms that were positively the pits.

Left to right: **Desert dunes** meet blue water at Face Canyon. **Kaibito Creek's** water-sculpted bed is a tributary of Navajo Canyon. **Flood-sculpted** sands and cliffs are reflected in Clear Creek Canyon. **Curls of dried mud** decorate a nameless Glen Canyon side canyon.

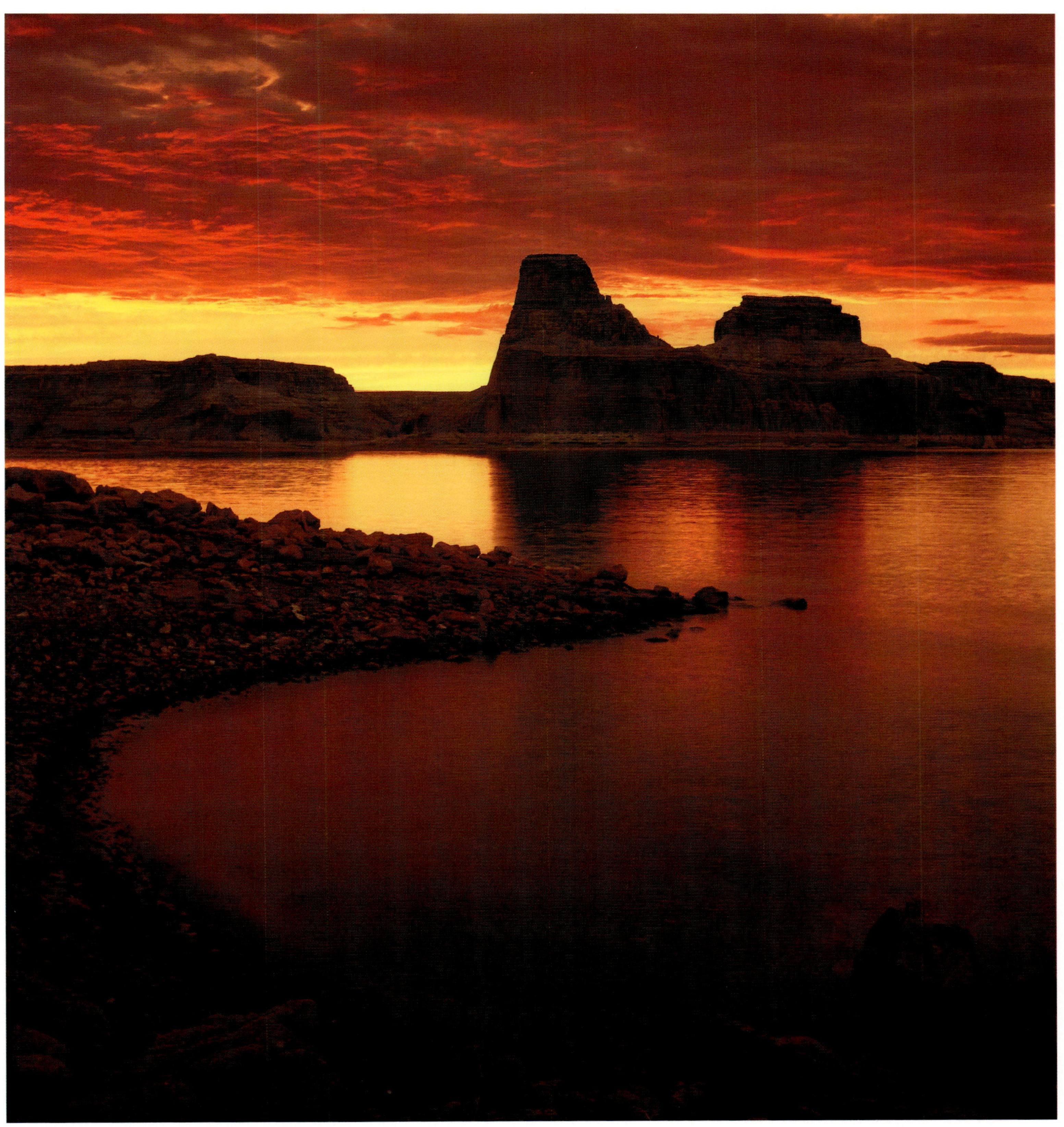

**A fiery August sunset** silhouettes Gunsight Butte on the north edge of Padre Bay. The old Colorado River followed a series of looping meanders through the stretch from West Canyon to Labyrinth Canyon. Lake Powell swallowed most of the meanders to create Padre Bay, which is up to five miles across.

## The Land

What makes this landscape so appealing? It's the curves, simple curves. Glen Canyon's tabular horizons are majestic and its rock layers orderly and systematic, but its details are definitely curvilinear. No superfluities, no annoying ornamentation, just elegant simplicity in curves

Here's what I see as a photographer in the Glen Canyon landscape: mosaics and patterns — parallel fingers of desert varnish, intricate parquets of sandstone cross-bedding, tessellated bedrock fracture patterns, irresistible diverging lines in its narrow-leaf yuccas, symmetric and asymmetric hollows and holes, ripple-marked mud and sand, and imbricated cobbles. In other words, *objets d'art* scattered throughout the Glen Canyon gallery, all connected by curving sandstone surfaces.

## The Lake

And what does a lake bring to such a landscape? Lake Powell is a fabulous convenience whose addition, unlike most conveniences, is not ugly. In fact, Lake Powell is a beautiful lake — not a power line or an irrigation ditch or an interstate highway littered with billboards. It may be artificial, but it's still inherently appealing.

Lake Powell, as seen from the air, is easily more photogenic than the Grand Canyon. Narrow arms of lake penetrate deep into the surrounding slickrock. The dark demeanor of the lake's waters contrast with the lighter tones of cradling rock. Even the "bathtub ring," usually perceived as an irritating flaw when viewed at close range, becomes an appealing corona when seen from above.

From the air, the incredible complexity of the ancient landscape and its upstart lake can be fully appreciated. You'll see slot canyons in every direction, beaches and campsites tucked into the most bizarre of locations, and peculiar land forms in confusing abundance.

Study the maze of slits and slots that surround Navajo Mountain and it becomes obvious why Rainbow Bridge was not revealed to the world until 1909. Consider the narrow parades of trees, bushes, and grasses that grow along a grid of bedrock fracture lines. Look at the dune forms in the sandy places. It's all quite preposterous. And from the air you'll realize that Lake Powell is no more than a puddle trapped in a universe of slickrock.

## The Landscape and the Lake

Keep this under your hat: Almost all visitors come to Lake Powell during the absolute worst possible time of year. They come in the summer when it's hot and crowded, when rental rates are highest and open campsite numbers are lowest. They come when the sun is too high and the nights are too short. They come when it's noisy and frantic. They come when the slick-rock flats have heated to incandescence.

Why? They come when the kids are out of school, when there are long holiday weekends, when the call of the wild is most audible. But they don't know what they're missing. It's during the off-season that Glen Canyon National Recreation Area is really on its game. The area reaches its zenith in charm and elegance when no one is around to be seduced by it. But, as I said, we don't need to draw attention to this fact. Let's leave well enough alone.

Glen Canyon National Recreation Area offers far more than a big lake. From its curvaceous cliffs, billowy sandstone domes, winding canyons, shapely arches, and sleek sandstone surfaces, Glen Canyon is a masterpiece of landscape sculpture that, by the way, also happens to have been joined by a nice little lake.

Right: **Kaibito Creek pours over limestone ledges** in Chaol Canyon where streaks of desert varnish reach down the cliffs to scattered cottonwood trees. Chaol Canyon is a tributary of Navajo Canyon. When Lake Powell rises to its maximum elevation, the edge of the lake arrives at the foot of this waterfall.

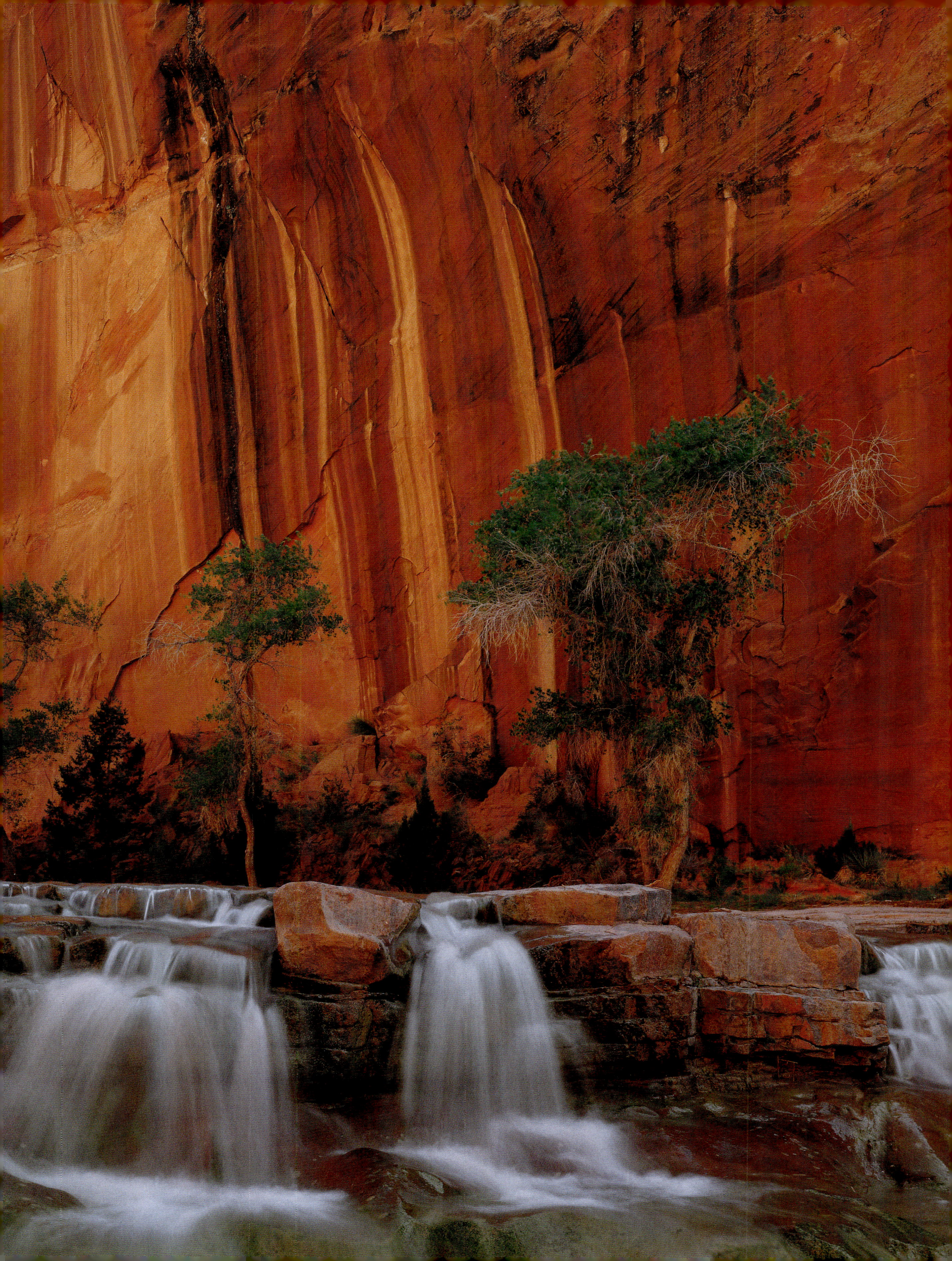

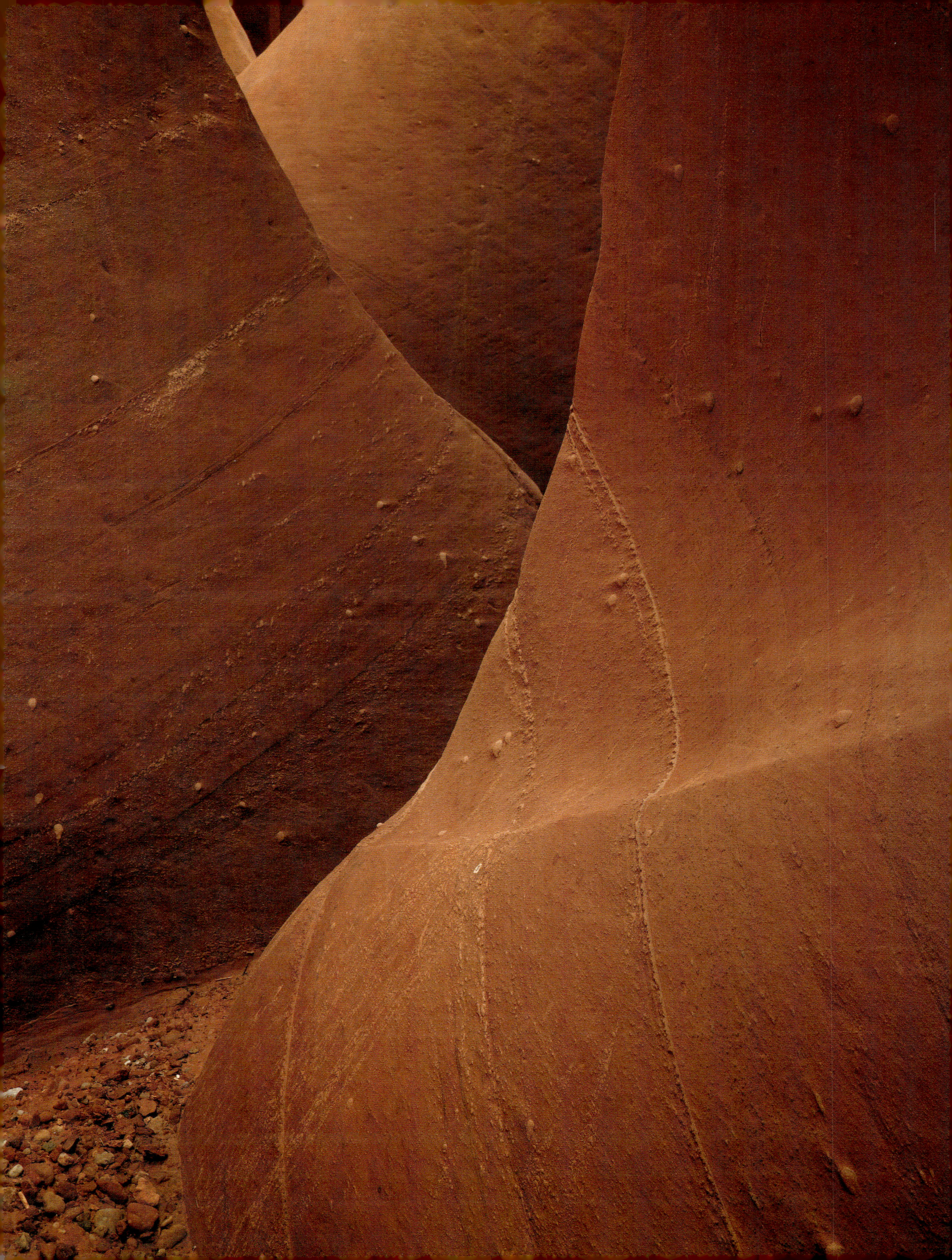

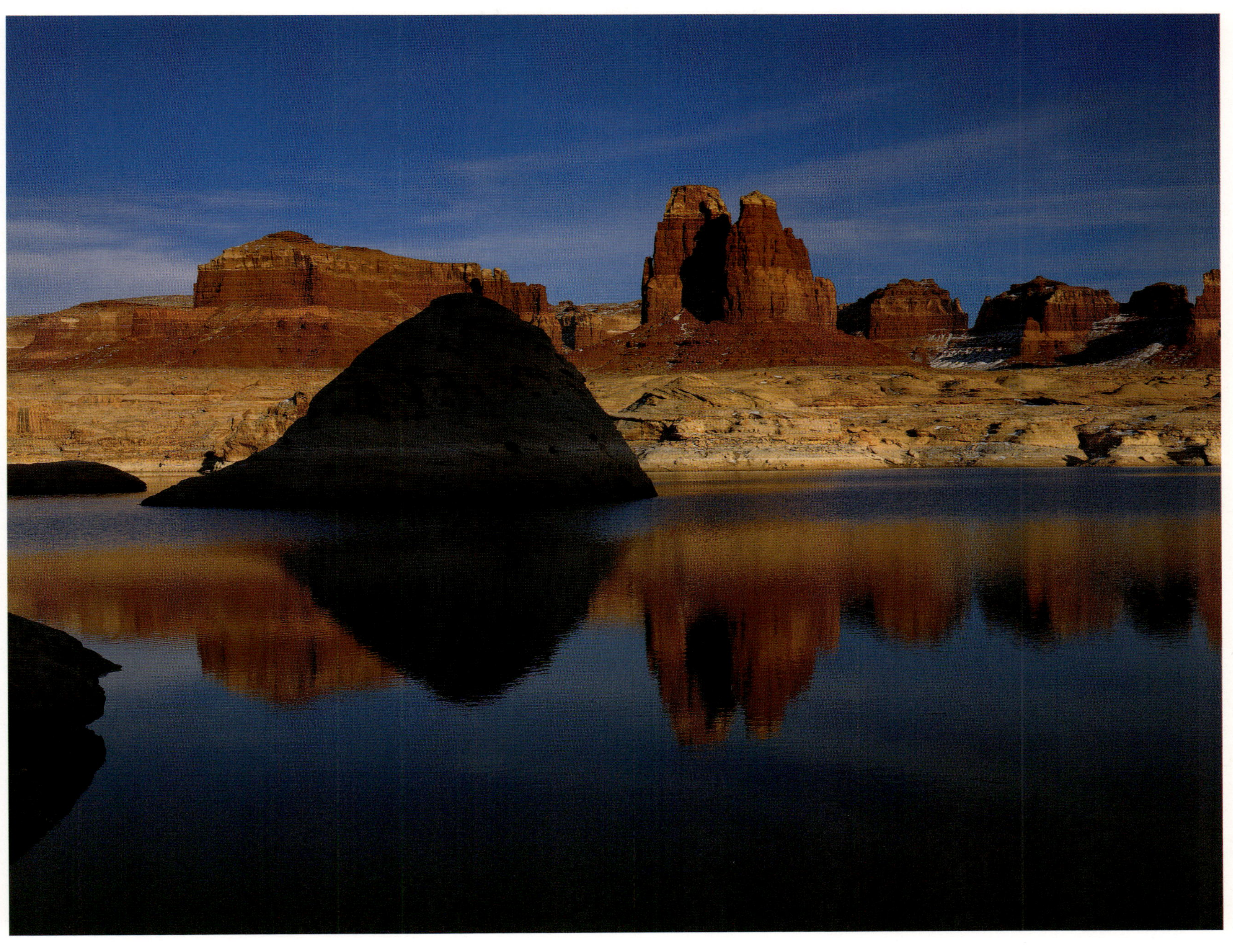

Left: **Interlocking walls of Navajo Sandstone** make walking this segment of Labyrinth Canyon somewhat like a drunken stagger. Diagonal lines in the sandstone define the downwind slopes of sand dunes that populated this area 190 million years ago.

Above: **Glen Canyon's rock** units rise toward the north end of the lake to expose deeper and older rock units at river and lake level. Grand Canyon-aged rocks line the shores of Lake Powell upstream from the mouth of the Dirty Devil River.

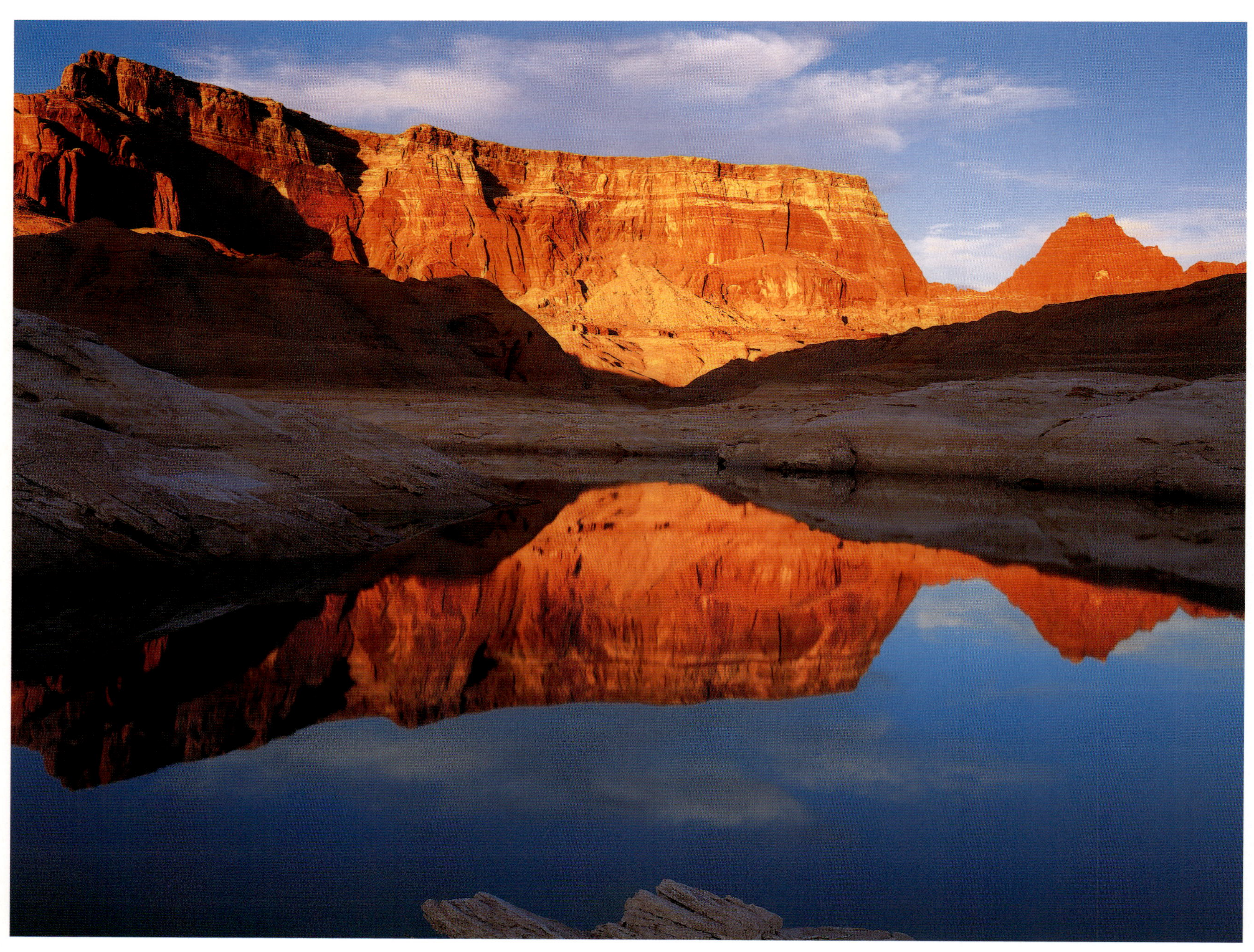

Above: **A March sunset** sets fire to a high mesa on the east side of Face Canyon. The upper end of Face Canyon is surrounded by cliffs 1,500 feet high.

Right: **Sandstone pinnacles and cliffs** catch the evening light in Fence Canyon, a tributary of Escalante Canyon. A small tamarisk turns from green to yellow as winter approaches.

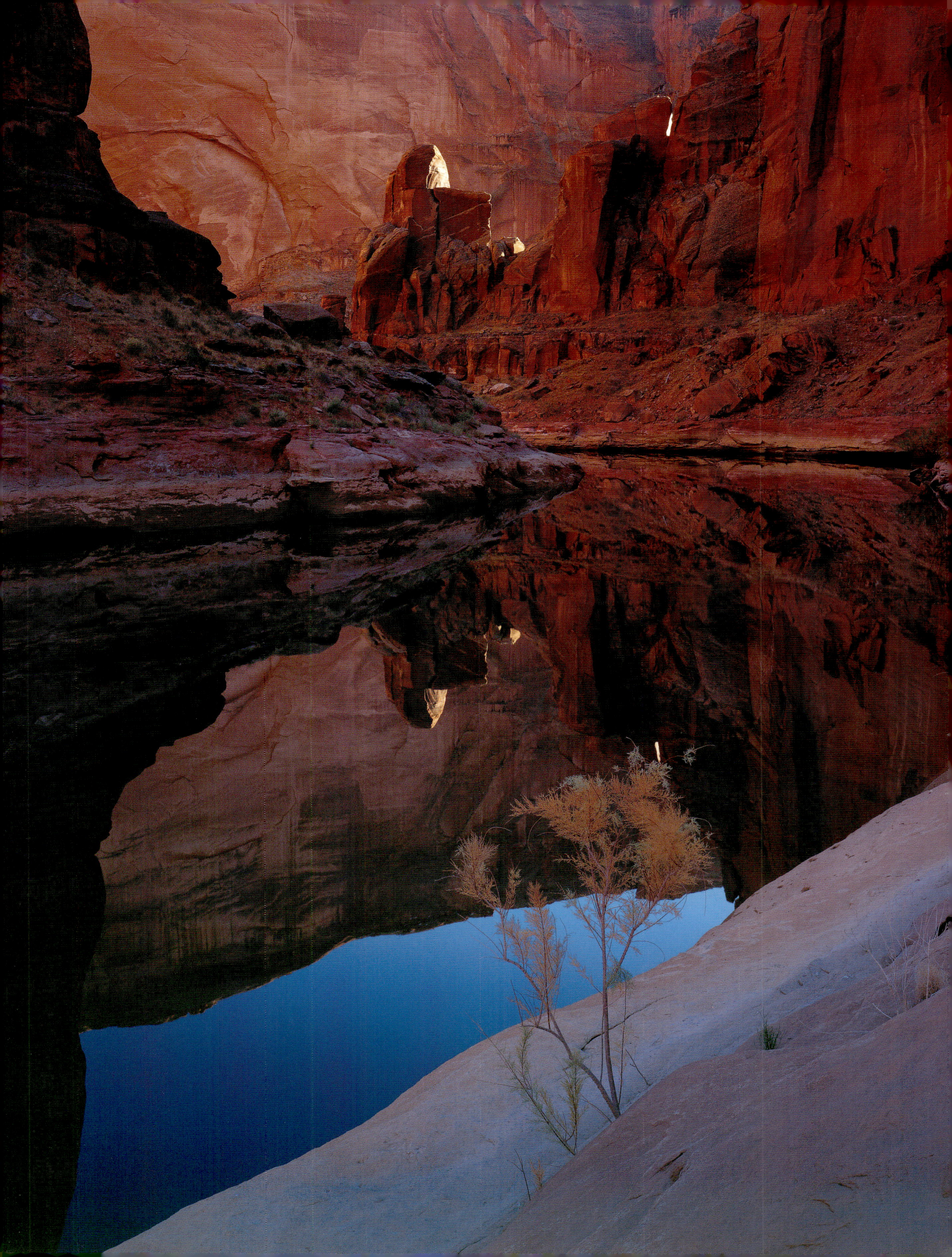

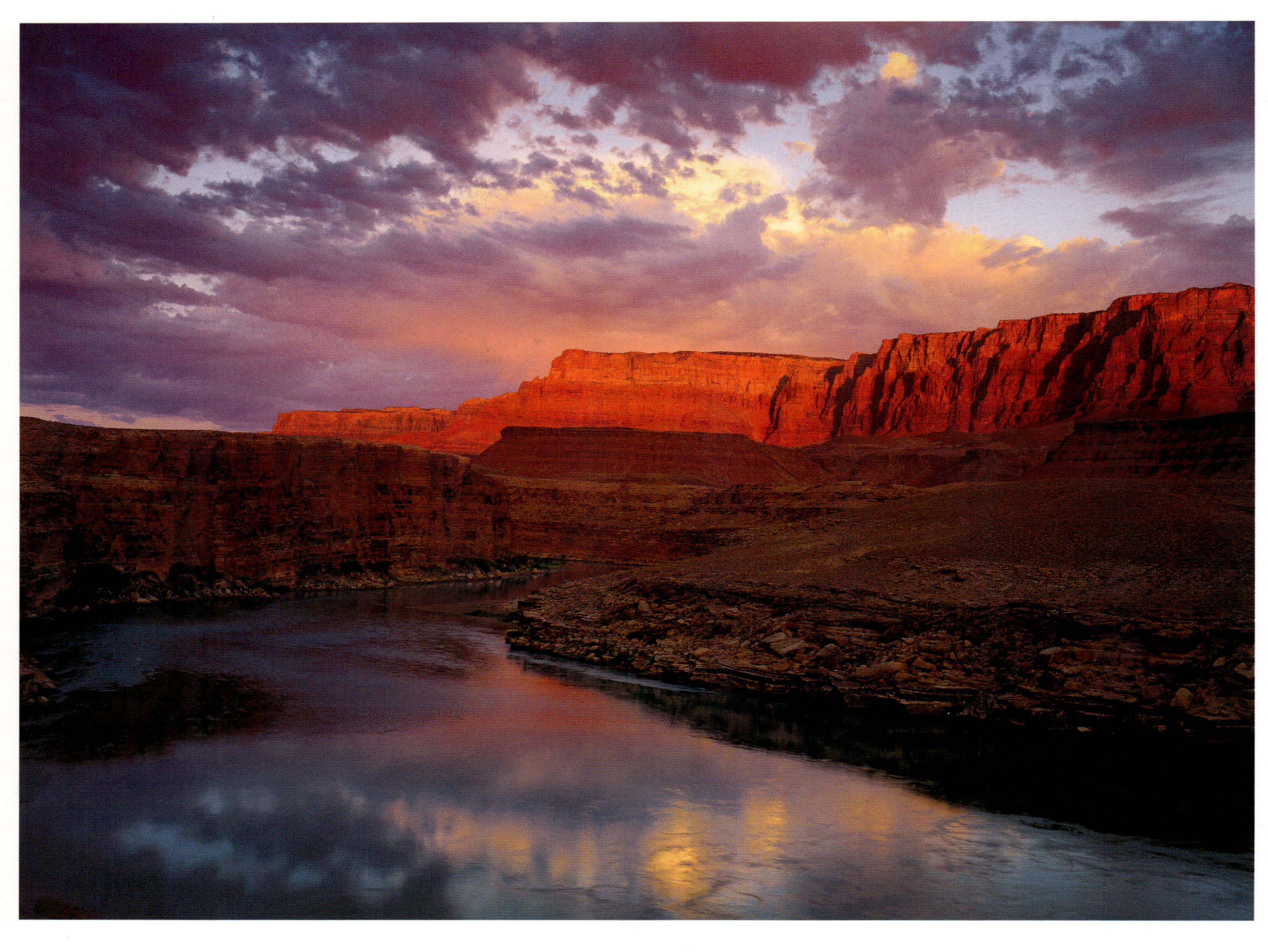

**Summer sunrise at Lee's Ferry** accents the majestic Vermilion Cliffs. In this view looking downstream from Lee's Ferry, the cliffs rise and retreat from the Colorado River, graciously surrendering their long and lovely Glen Canyon reign.

# Services and Information

**Glen Canyon National Recreation Area** is large and complex, with dozens of services and scores of supporting businesses inside and outside its boundaries.

## Administration

**National Park Service/Glen Canyon National Recreation Area and Rainbow Bridge National Monument**, www.nps.gov/glca.

**Carl Hayden Visitor Center** near Page, AZ:

- **National Park Service**, (928) 608-6404.
- **Bookstore (Glen Canyon Natural History Association)**, (928) 608-6068.
- **Glen Canyon Dam tours** (reservations & information), (928) 608-6072.

**Bullfrog Visitor Center** near Bullfrog, UT, (435) 684-7423.

**Park Headquarters** at Page, AZ, (928) 608-6200.

**Navajo Bridge Interpretive Center**, Marble Canyon, AZ, (928) 355-2319.

**Volunteer Programs: The Trash Tracker program and the Graffiti Removal program,** (928) 608-6350.

## Museums and Educational Organizations

**Glen Canyon Natural History Association** (GCNRA's nongovernmental partner manages visitors center bookstores, co-sponsors lectures of local interest, manages public tours of Glen Canyon Dam, etc), www.glencanyonnha.org.

- **Main office** at Page, AZ, (877) GLEN-CYN
- **Bookstore** at Glen Canyon Dam, (928) 608-6068.

**Grand Circle Field School** (GCNRA's nongovernmental partner for educational trips within the recreation area including Elderhostel houseboat-supported adventures.) Headquarters for educational houseboat, kayak, and hiking trips, 505-797-8540, www.grandcirclefieldschool.org.

**John Wesley Powell Museum** in Page, AZ. Museum of Colorado River river-running, history of Glen Canyon Dam and Page paleontology and more, (928) 645-9496, www.powellmuseum.org.

## Page/Lake Powell Chamber of Commerce

475 S. Lake Powell Blvd., C-4,
(928) 645-2741,
www.pagelakepowellchamber.org.

## Page/Lake Powell Tourism Bureau

647-A Elm Street
(888) 261-PAGE or (928) 660-3405,
www.pagelakepowelltourism.com.

## Navajo Village Heritage Center

Northeast corner of State Route 98 and Coppermine Road, (928) 660-0304
www.navajo-village.com.

## General Web Site Information on the Lake Powell Area

**Lake Powell Life**, local business directory, diners guide and more, www.lakepowelllife.com.

**Rivers and Oceans**, Grand Canyon river trips departing Lee's Ferry and more, www.rivers-oceans.com.

**Grand Canyon and Lake Powell area information and booking services**, www.grandcanyon.com.

**Utah's largest travel site, information on Lake Powell**, www.go-utah.com/lake-powell.

**Lake Powell Guide**, Page, AZ, and Lake Powell information, *Lake Powell* Magazine, www. powellguide.com.

## Marinas

**ARAMARK is the largest concessionaire within Glen Canyon National Recreation Area. It operates four marinas within the park, including Wahweap Marina near Page, AZ, the park's largest and most complete marina complex, www.lakepowell.com.**

- **Boat rental center for all Aramark marinas**, (800) 528-6154, (928) 645-2433 for local calls.
- **Wahweap boat tour trips**, (800) 528-6154, (928) 645-1070 for local calls.
- **Wahweap's Lake Powell Resort**, (800) 204-0623, (928) 645-2433 for local calls.
- **Bullfrog Marina**, UT, recorded information, (435) 684-3000.
- **Bullfrog's Defiance House Lodge**, UT, (435) 684-3032.
- **Bullfrog's boat maintenance shop**, UT, (435) 684-3008.
- **Hall's Crossing Marina**, UT, recorded information, (435) 684-7000.
- **Hall's Crossing Marina Store**, UT, (435) 684-7028.
- **Hall's Crossing Village Center RV Park**, UT, (435) 684-7009.

**FOREVER RESORTS is the second-largest park concessionaire. It operates Antelope Point Marina, Lake Powell's newest marina, www.antelopepointlakepowell.com.**

- **General information number and directory for Ja' di' tooh**, floating restaurant and lounge, retail store, dry storage, lake excursions and guided-group lake tours, launch and retrieve service, guest transfers from the Page airport, catering and more, (928) 645-5900.
- **Boat rental reservations**, (800) 255-5561.

## Boat Trips on the Colorado River Downstream from the Dam

**Colorado River Discovery**, downstream one-day river trips or transporting boat gear from Lee's Ferry to near the base of the dam, 130 6th Avenue, Page, AZ, (928) 645-9175 and (888) 522-6644, www.coriverdiscovery.com.

## Scenic Flights from the Page Airport

**Westwind Aviation**, (928) 645-2494, www.westwindaviation.com.

**American Aviation**, (928) 608-1060, www.americanaviationwest.com.

**Classic Aviation**, jet & helicopter charters, (928) 645-5356, (800) 444-9220, www.classicaviation.net.

## Regularly Scheduled Commercial Flights to Page, AZ

**Great Lakes Airlines**, Page Airport, (928) 645-1355; reservations (800) 554-5111; www.greatlakesav.com.

## Page Area Slot Canyon Tours

**Antelope Canyon Navajo Tours**, at Upper Antelope Canyon, (928) 698-3384 or (928) 698-3285, www.navajotours.com.

**Antelope Canyon Tours**, 22 S. Lake Powell Blvd., (928) 645-9102, www.antelopecanyon.com.

**Antelope Slot Canyon Tours by Chief Tsosie**, 55 S. Lake Powell Blvd., www.antelopeslotcanyon.com.

**Overland Canyon Tours**, 48 S. Lake Powell Blvd., inside Thunderbird Art Gallery, (Antelope Canyon, Canyon X and Vermilion Cliffs National Monument), (928) 608-4072, www.overlandcanyontours.com.

**Slot Canyon Hummer Adventures**, 12 Lake Powell Blvd., (928) 645-2266, www.hummeradventures.net.

## Page Area Jeep Rentals and More

**Canyon Country Adventures**, 695 N. Navajo Drive, jeep, boat and pwc rentals, (928) 645-4004, www.ccadventures.net.

## Guided Fishing Services on the Colorado River

**Lee's Ferry Anglers Guides and Fly Shop, Marble Canyon, AZ**, (800) 962-9755 or (928) 355-2261, www.leesferry.com.

**Marble Canyon Outfitters, Marble Canyon, AZ**, (800) 533-7339 or (928) 645-9235, www.leesferryflyfishing.com.

## Guided Fishing Services on Lake Powell

**Ambassador Guides and Outfitters**, Page, AZ, (Lake Powell & Lee's Ferry), (928) 645-0057, www.ambassadorguides.com.

**McNabb Fishing Guide Service**, Page, AZ, (928) 645-5122, www.mcnabbfishingguideservice.com.

**This Side of That Guide Service**, Page, AZ, (928) 660-0136.

## Lake Powell Fishing Information

www.wayneswords.com.

## Guided Hiking Services

**Escalante Canyon Outfitters**, Boulder, UT. Hiking adventures in southern Utah, (888) 326-4453, www.ecohike.com.

**Far Out Expeditions**, Bluff, UT. Day tours of Monument Valley, Cedar Mesa and Grand Gulch, 435-672-2294, www.faroutexpeditions.com.

## Guided Kayak Services

**Glen Canyon Kayak Guides/Kayak** L.P., Page, AZ, (888) 854-7862.

**Hidden Canyon Kayak**, Page, AZ. Full-day and multiday kayak adventures on Lake Powell, (800) 343-3121 or (928) 645-8866, www.hiddencanyonkayak.com.

## Page Area Photo Stores

**Foto Quick/The Portrait Place**, 644 N. Navajo Drive, (928) 645-5360.

**Walmart SuperCenter 1-Hour Photo**, State Route 89 at 1017 W. Haul Road, (928) 645-4930.

## Page Area Boating Club

**Lake Powell Yacht Club**, 818 Aqua Ave., (928) 645-3992, www.lpyachtclub.org.

## Page Area Navajo Trading Posts

**Big Lake Trading Post,** 1501 Highway 98 (State Route 98) at Coppermine Road, (928) 645-2404.

**Blair's Trading Post**, 626 N. Navajo Drive, (928) 645-3008, www.blairstradingpost.com.

**Pow Wow Trading Post**, 635 Elm St., (928) 645-2140, www.powwowtrading.com.

## Page Area Super Store

**Walmart SuperCenter**, with grocery, 1-hour photo, pharmacy, tire & lube, on U.S. Route 89 at 1017 W. Haul Road. General information, (928) 645-2622.

## Vessel Repair Services

**Aquanuts, Inc.**, Big Water, UT, (435) 675-9161.

**Canyon Boat Works**, Page, AZ, (928) 645-5549.

**Crazy Needle Canvas**, Page, AZ, (928) 645-2811.

**Desert Service, Inc.**, Page, AZ, (928) 608-0128.

**Lake Powell Marine**, Page, AZ, (928) 645-2592.

**Old West Marine Services, Inc.**, Page, AZ, (928) 645-2705, www.oldwestmarine.com.

**Ray's Upholstery**, Page, AZ, (928) 645-3537.

**Tony's Dri Dock 7 Marine**, Page, AZ, (928) 645-2732.

**Triple L. Marine, L.L.C.**, Page, AZ, (928) 645-2669, http://triplelmarine.com.

**Unlimited Houseboat Services**, Page, AZ, (928) 645-4060, www.uhshouseboats.com.

# Photo Tips

*Tips for Photographing Lake Powell and Glen Canyon National Recreation Area*

**These are not technical tips, which can be found in many photo books, but are my own philosophical tips that point the way toward improved photographs of Lake Powell and the surrounding landscape. — *Gary Ladd***

## Have Patience

There are times when a photographer scrambles to grab a shot of an ephemeral waterfall plunging into the lake after a summer cloudburst, or the moving beam of sunshine just now spotlighting Tower Butte. Far more often, however, it is patience, not speed, that's required for capturing powerful images. On the water or on the slickrock around the lake, I try to be vigilant because I know that most worthy photos must be *stalked*. I must search them out. A great photo may be hiding around the next bend, but I won't catch it if I'm snoozing on my beach towel.

## Zero in on Details

What would it be like to live your life without the ability to see anything up close? Cliffs and clouds and mountains would be available but never a wildflower, a pretty stone, or a baby's hand. It would be a life without intimacies — a tragedy. That's why you'll always want to include close-ups in your photographic repertoire. Universes teeming with photo possibilities can be found in close-ups. Plants, cobbles, ripple marks, and footprints in the sand are some of the inhabitants. Don't let the grandeur of the huge trample the beauty of the small.

## Gaze at Reflections

I'm usually one of the last to adopt the latest technology. Over the years I've been dragged into zoom lenses, forced into autofocus, and beaten down by digital capture. So, it wasn't until I took up zoom lenses, autofocus, and auto-exposure that one type of Lake Powell photography became possible. I'm referring to telephoto images of reflections of cliff and sky on slick water that's been distorted by a boat wake. The abstract patterns that emerge from this technique can be sensational. Use fast shutter speeds and keep shooting as the scenes evolve from moment to moment. Erase those (there will be many) that don't measure up.

## Populate With People

It has taken me a long time, but I've finally learned that the presence of the human figure in landscape photos is often a key element. A sense of scale is one reason. The grand landscapes around Lake Powell are so vast and surreal that it helps to include a human figure for comparison. But there are other advantages — the introduction of a new palette of color, the creation of a point of focus, the information or mood conveyed by body language, and, if it is an action scene, the action itself (hiking, working, paddling, etc.) is half the story.

## Honor the Gifts

By being patient and vigilant, and by looking carefully, photographers are rewarded with nature's gifts. These pretty presents may contain an afternoon of beautiful clouds, a flower in bloom in a side canyon, or a compelling pattern of rippled sand. The gift is incomplete, however, until the photographer ties a "ribbon" on the package. I mean that it is the photographer's responsibility to render the gift irresistibly pleasing to the eye by adding an interesting composition, proper exposure, and careful timing. Otherwise, the photographer is just a passive collector, not an artist, not a true photographer.

## Find Forceful Foregrounds

Lake Powell routinely offers awesome backdrops of orange cliffs, imposing buttes and splendid plateaus. I will consider recording such a scene if the light is right ... and after I check what's in front of my toes that can be employed as a pleasing foreground. Is there a cactus in bloom, an interesting pattern of rippled beach sand, or an angular slab of rock jutting over the water? A compelling image with a forceful foreground is most often captured with a wide-angle lens to gain greater depth of focus and a three-dimensional aspect.

## Employ Technical Options

Don't forget to consider the use of the many photographic options at your disposal. For each scene that you find attractive, apply those techniques that flatter the situation the most. Choose the time of day and sun angle: direct sun, shade, or cloud shadows. Should the sky be included in the frame? Which is best, horizontal or vertical format? Is a fast or slow shutter speed desirable? Large or small aperture? Lens focal length? Every photo can be improved or degraded by a photographer's decisions. Never let the decision be made by default.

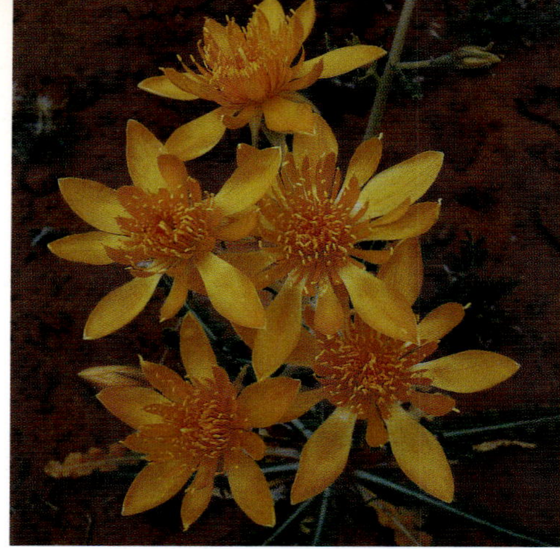

Blooming stickleaf

## Seek Counterpoints

Many photographs are extra-effective if they include counterpoints or elements that are opposites. Here are some examples: a bright green plant surrounded by red sandstone, a delicate flower growing amid rugged boulders, a compelling pattern or symmetry that also includes a flaw in the symmetry, or a perfectly round object lost in a field of angular objects. Such scenes are usually close-ups or semi-close-ups, and they are usually invisible to photographers who are too easily wowed by the grand scale of Lake Powell's majestic buttes and mesas.

## Turn Wide Views on Their Sides

I never use wide-angle lenses to squeeze in as much of Lake Powell and its sandstone surroundings as possible. Wide views will crush the grand cliffs and buttes into insignificance. Instead, I find an interesting foreground like a slickrock pool or a group of cobbles at lake's edge, I move in close, and I use a vertical format. The grand distant cliffs thus become a useful backdrop. Used in this way, I sometimes call the wide-angle lens a "two-directional" lens because it can simultaneously gaze down on appealing foregrounds and out toward distances dominated by the vertical. Surfaces that face in different directions offer pleasingly diverse colors and features.

## Look Even Deeper

One of the benefits of making photographs within one landscape for dozens of years is that the photographer gradually creates a body of effective images that additional work will only repeat. Having finally bagged a fine image, I might feel that I'm finished at one particular location. But not so fast. On my next visit I must look deeper, look more carefully to see what I missed earlier while I was so single-mindedly focused on the original idea. I literally ask myself questions: What else is here? What if I change focal lengths or if I get down lower or up higher or work under a cloudy sky? What have I missed by being so committed to getting that one view?

### Admire the Clouds

Clouds are pure magic. The skies over Lake Powell are often clear, so when the clouds move in I automatically flip on my "Very Vigilant" switch that considers how these gifts can be utilized. Clouds add interest to the sky; they throw light into the shaded areas (reducing contrast); they randomly paint the distances with shadows (emphasizing depth); they tweak a scene's color balance; and when they fall upon the photographer they usually improve close-up photographs by bathing the subject (a flower, a lizard, a lichen, a group of stones) with a gentle diffuse light. I absolutely never ignore clouds over Lake Powell.

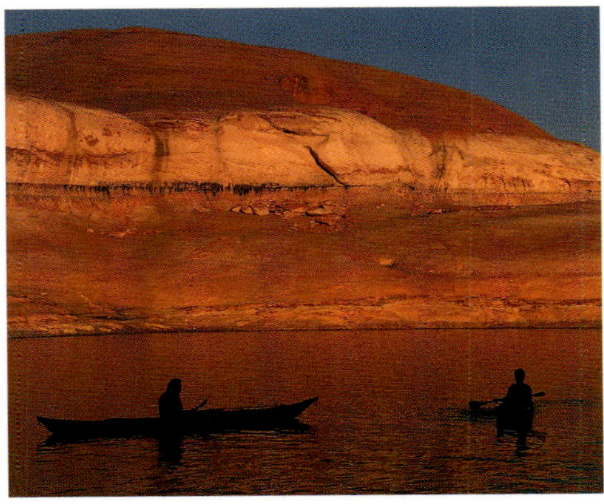

### Search Silhouettes and Shadows

We humans tend to focus on those areas that are in direct sunlight and not notice what's contained within shaded areas, or more importantly, the shapes of those shaded areas. But there are great photos embedded in shadows and silhouettes. I force myself to see shadow shapes (above right), and sometimes I'm rewarded with photos that are simple and effective. I also look for silhouettes of people, trees, and boats against a bright sky or sunlit cliff (above). And I look for the elongated shadows of hikers moving across a clean slate of slickrock.

### Appreciate the Commonplace

Physicists studying the nature of reality have said that their goal is not so much to see what others have never seen but to fully understand that which everybody sees but fails to appreciate. It's the same for photographers. It is my hope that I'm alert to promising situations that others, even if they are standing next to me, will not recognize. It's not so much the once-in-a-lifetime fiery sunset or the rare fifty-bloom cactus that I hope to capture, it's the commonplace that I hope to perceive and record as uncommonly interesting. Of course, lesser images made along the way will be welcomed also.

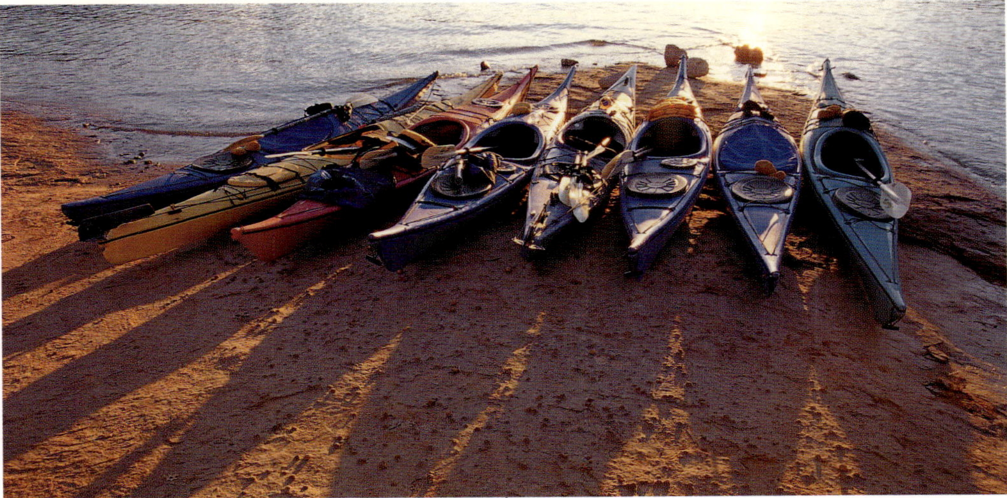

# Safety Principles for Lake Powell

My home in Page is located beneath the helicopter approach to the local hospital. In the summer when the lake is busy with boaters, helicopter flights transporting injured vacationers to the hospital are common, each one signaling a sad end to someone's Lake Powell visit.

Please help keep my neighborhood quiet and your Lake Powell experience wonderful by observing these eight safety principles:

1. While boating, maintain safe and reasonable distances from all other vessels and stationary obstacles.
2. Never drink and pilot a boat.
3. Never boat at night.
4. Ensure that all children ages 12 and younger wear personal flotation devices whenever they are passengers in speedboats and anytime they are near the water.
5. Always be cautious of carbon monoxide poisoning whenever boat generators and engines are running. (Swimming while unknowingly breathing carbon monoxide fumes is a swift and deadly combination.)
6. Maintain parental control and oversight of children on land and lake.
7. Require that all swimmers be accompanied by swimming buddies.
8. While swimming, never approach a boat while its motor is running.

In general, keep in mind that your boating world on Lake Powell is nowhere near as familiar as your home environment. Hazards can be easily overlooked. Keep alert and keep calculating what *could* happen if..."

*— Gary Ladd*

### Preventing Quagga and Zebra Mussels

Quagga and zebra mussels from eastern Europe were inadvertently introduced into the Great Lakes in the 1980s. They have since spread westward, clogging lake water intake pipes, drains, engine cooling systems, and aqueducts, while degrading water quality and clarity and fouling beaches. They have caused a plague of severe economic and ecological damage.

In their larval stages, quagga and zebra mussels are microscopic, rendering them difficult to spot and eliminate. It is your responsibility to be certain your boat and trailer do not bring invasive mussels to Lake Powell from other infested waters.

National Park Service rangers will inspect your boat and trailer when you enter the recreation area, and you may be required to decontaminate your equipment at a specialized boat-washing area.

To help protect Lake Powell, here's what to do:

- Before leaving any lake, drain all the water from the boat, including the live well and lower unit.
- Clean the hull to remove all mud, plant and animal material.
- Air-dry the boat for at least five days before launching in another body of water.
- Be prepared to carry out further inspections and treatments as required, especially if you have boated in infested waters in the last 30 days.

For the latest information about halting the spread of quagga and zebra mussels, visit the Arizona Game and Fish Department online at www.azgfd.gov/mussels, and the National Park Service Glen Canyon National Recreation Area online at www.nps.gov/glca.

# Index